THE
BRUTALITY
OF WAR

THE
BRUTALITY OF WAR

A MEMOIR OF VIETNAM

Gene R. Dark

iUniverse, Inc.
New York Lincoln Shanghai

The Brutality of War
A Memoir of Vietnam

iUniverse books may be ordered through booksellers or by contacting:

iUniverse
2021 Pine Lake Road, Suite 100
Lincoln, NE 68512
www.iuniverse.com
1-800-Authors (1-800-288-4677)

Because of the dynamic nature of the Internet, any Web addresses or links contained in this book may have changed since publication and may no longer be valid.

The views expressed in this work are solely those of the author and do not necessarily reflect the views of the publisher, and the publisher hereby disclaims any responsibility for them.

ISBN: 978-0-595-45893-6 (pbk)
ISBN: 978-0-595-69749-6 (cloth)
ISBN: 978-0-595-90194-4 (ebk)

Printed in the United States of America

In memory of Harmon J. Bove Jr.

Man is the only animal that deals in that atrocity of atrocities, War. He is the only one that gathers his brethren about him and goes forth in cold blood and calm pulse to exterminate his kind. He is the only animal that for sordid wages will march out ... and help to slaughter strangers of his own species who have done him no harm and with whom he has no quarrel ... And in the intervals between campaigns he washes the blood off his hands and works for "the universal brotherhood of man"—with his mouth.

—Mark Twain, "What Is Man?"

Acknowledgments

My gratitude goes out to all the marines I served with in Vietnam. I thank my drill instructors, who made me a man, and Dwight Anderson, my squad leader in Vietnam, for trusting and believing in me. Anderson was also instrumental in helping me remember certain events, names, and places that were clouded by the "fog of war."

I thank Davis Brown, author of *Battlelines*, a book about Fox Company, Second Battalion, Fifth Marines. By writing the book, he unknowingly helped me sort out events that I participated in while serving in Vietnam but was unable to remember accurately.

This book is for all who have served this great country on the battlefield, and especially for Harmon J. Bove Jr., a friend, a man, and a great marine who died fighting for America.

To my friend Claude Duet, a friend and mentor who encouraged me throughout the writing of this book.

Thank you to my mother and father for loving me enough to teach me right from wrong. And thanks to my sisters, Allison, Eve, and Margaret, for supporting me through the years when I needed it most.

With great love and gratitude I thank my wife, Nettie, sons, Brian and Beau, and my lovely daughter, Jennifer, who all continued to love me through the good times and bad.

Prologue

It is well that war is so terrible; or we should get too fond of it.

—Robert E. Lee

I was a marine. I was assigned to Fox Company, Second Battalion, Fifth Marines. Fox 2/5 was one of the most decorated marine companies that served in Vietnam. I still love the Marine Corps; everything it stands for is honorable, as were the marines who I served with. I wasn't special in any way. I was just a young kid. I wasn't brave, and I wasn't proud of some of the things I did. I was cast as a leader not by choice but by default. I was a grunt, an infantryman, a fire team leader, promoted to squad leader, and then promoted to platoon sergeant. Then, for the last few months of my tour in Vietnam, I was promoted to NCOIC (noncommissioned officer in charge) of Fox Company Headquarters in An Hoa, Vietnam. I was meritoriously promoted three times, once when I graduated from boot camp and then twice while in Vietnam, where I was meritoriously combat promoted. I went from being a private to a corporal in a little over thirteen months.

I never considered myself brave or worthy of praise for anything that I did. Others were much braver than I was. In my mind, I had failed so many times. Even if others weren't aware of it at the time, I often felt like a coward inside. After thirty-seven years removed from my war, I still remain in awe of the marines that I served with in Vietnam and the valor they displayed.

The rain, mud, heat, and disease of that third-world country were horrendous. I was hospitalized for immersion foot and malaria. I survived the notorious mosquitoes of Vietnam from July 1969 to July 1970. My poncho was my home—it kept me dry during the monsoon and shielded me from the relentless sun in the summer.

I saw death. I know and understand the terror of the firefight, with rifle rounds zinging past my head, filling the air. Once you have experienced an ambush you never forget it. I know what it's like to feel the heartache of losing a fellow marine. I've looked down the sights of a rifle barrel and stared into the eyes of the enemy, coldly pulling the trigger and killing him. I am still haunted by the image. Killing is not something to boast about.

Even though I never thought highly of my abilities, I guess others recognized my potential, since I scored 4.8 out of a possible 5.0 when judged by my superiors for conduct and proficiency. As the marines would say, "I had my shit together." I received the Purple Heart, the National Defense Medal, the Navy Commendation Medal, the Combat Action Medal, the Vietnam Service Medal, the Republic of Vietnam Cross of Gallantry Medal, and a Sharpshooter Badge.

These are my memoirs of war. I have no agenda other than telling the truth about war. I hope you will feel the same emotions that lie deep within me and perhaps understand how war can so deeply impact the young soldiers that we ask to protect America, many of whom are mere children.

I love America. I volunteered to serve my country and specifically to serve as a marine. I wasn't drafted; I joined out of pride for America and what it stands for. I am a patriot. It matters not which war one fought; the emotions of battle are all the same.

Ask any soldier who has walked point while leading a column of tough marines during a night movement, deep into the heart of the enemy's territory, and he will always remember that night. It's just that frightening of an experience. He moves slowly, sweating profusely as he waits to see the flash of the rifle muzzle aimed right between his eyes, and fears the horrifying, unmistakable cracking sound of AK-47s firing on automatic—KAK-KAK-KAK—whizzing by his head, slamming into the ground around him. Yes, he will remember that night forever.

Or he nervously awaits the blast from an explosive device under his foot, which will shatter his limbs, blowing him away, maiming and crippling as many other soldiers as possible. He is alone, out front, by himself, exposed, naked except for his flak jacket and helmet. He asks himself, "Who is faster or smarter tonight, me or the enemy?" Alone with his demons, fighting to maintain his sanity and not to be exposed as a coward, he moves forward—honor, duty, country—bravely he moves, creeping, one step after the other. He was hurled into a situation for which no amount of training could have prepared him.

Is it any wonder that man is so affected by war? War is typically fought by naïve kids who get thrown into battle and are subjected to the most horrendous acts imaginable. Then we wonder why Johnny is a little different when he returns home. Why is he so quiet? Even if he is lucky enough not to be reminded of war by a missing limb that was blown off his body when he stepped on a mine, or a scar across his belly where shrapnel ripped him open, or a hole in his leg where a bullet found its mark that fateful day on the battlefield—even if he is that lucky—his mind remains warped with dreams. The stench, taste, grit, and dread of war never leaves his mind, and the years drift by while the memories remain.

The fog of war is real. I've tried to recall events that happened during war as accurately as possible, but sometimes I'm not sure if my memories are real or imaginary. I don't remember names very well either. Maybe forgetting your buddies' names protects your sanity when they got blown away. Yet, I have never bonded so strongly with anyone as with a fellow marine that I served with in combat. I tell myself that it was just a long time ago, but I know there is more to it than forgetfulness.

When in war, the soldier's brain insulates him from the painful memories, not allowing him to keep experiencing the pain night after night. I once had a reoccurring dream. I don't have it anymore, but for years it haunted me.

I dreamed that I was sitting in my foxhole on a nondescript hill in Vietnam. My position overlooks a rice paddy five hundred meters away. The monsoon fog lays low. The clouds are dark and a light, misty rain falls; it's late afternoon and will be dark soon. An eerie quiet falls on the growing darkness and the heavy, humid air smothers me like a rain-soaked blanket.

In my peripheral vision I see a marine in the distance. He is walking point, holding his rifle in front of his chest, finger on the trigger, burdened with his gear, glancing from side to side as he emerges from the brush. Reluctantly, he begins to cross the open ground to continue the patrol. Cautiously he advances, taking precise steps, then motions for the rest of the marines to follow. In single file, one after another, they emerge from the tree line, advancing across the paddy dike toward their objective: a hill only a few hundred meters away. Just as the point man reaches the high ground, an explosion rips the still evening. Dirt and mud fly into the air, and I feel the concussion of the explosion from hundreds of meters away. The marines freeze.

When they realize what has happened, they emerge from the shock and start running to help their fallen marines. Another explosion rings out, then another. The enemy did well setting their trap. A series of mines rips the flesh of the young marines. The confusion sets in once again. Will their next step trigger another explosion? The squad leader grabs a marine humping the radio, grasps the radio headset, and calls for a medivac chopper. The other marines dash about to form a perimeter to defend the chopper already on its way from Da Nang in a race to save the wounded marines.

Within a few minutes a yellow smoke is thrown by a marine onto the LZ to give the wind direction to the circling chopper. The thumping blades beat the air, signaling the arrival of two attack choppers, which fly around the LZ occasionally firing into the brush to discourage the Vietcong from attacking the medivac chopper. Then, like a rock, the chopper drops, freefalling from the clouds onto the side of the hill. The back door of the chopper flies open and the wounded walls, oorah and oorah! I know you have to get pumped and ready to kill before battle or else you won't win, but it is still hard for me to watch knowing what's in store for those kids, who are barely old enough to drink a beer. I know there will come a day when each of those soldiers will be sitting in their living room, some looking down at a stump where a once-strong leg used to be that he lost on the battle-field, and they will ask themselves: Was fighting for America worth the sacrifice?

Chapter 1

There is nothing that war has ever achieved that we could not bet-ter achieve without it.

—William Hooke

In 1995, I stood daydreaming in front of my office window, staring at the threatening skies, mesmerized by the trees whipping violently in the gusting wind. It would be raining much harder soon. I wore the look of a haggard man. My hair was graying and my starched collar of my perfectly creased white shirt squeezed my neck tightly and my red silk tie hung loosely down to my belt buckle. Everything in my office was perfectly arranged, a byproduct of being a marine. I saw my reflec-tion in the glass, revealing the deepening lines in my once youthful face. I was almost forty-five and twenty-five years had passed since leav-ing Vietnam. I walked back to my desk and sank into my soft brown leather chair.

On the wall behind my desk hung a picture of my oldest son in his dress blue marine uniform, and next to it sat a shadow box of medals I had earned in Vietnam, with a picture of myself as a youthful marine sitting under my poncho in the jungle in 1969. Only nineteen when the picture was taken, I appeared to be more child than man. I could hardly believe that it was me. Sitting under my poncho, poised with my rifle, shirtless except for my flak jacket, and lying on my pack which held everything that I owned in life, I was ready for battle. I remember it was taken in the Arizona Territory, a notorious area in Vietnam. The picture was a vivid reminder that no matter how tough life got or how bleak my situation appeared to be in my current life, I needed only glance at the photo to remind me of where I had been, what I had endured, and how brutal life could really get, and suddenly my everyday problems became meaningless.

My son had quickly grown into a man and joined the Marine Corps; I'm sure that I influenced his decision. On a recent trip to attend his Marine Corps graduation ceremony in San Diego, I realized that all the emotions of being a marine were once again stirring inside of me. Watching those fine young stallions being molded into men, hearing the familiar screaming by the drill instructors, and seeing the red and gold colors proudly displayed everywhere filled my heart with an old, buried pride of being a marine. Only another marine understands the power of the corps, of being marine. Semper Fi says it all. For the next few days, I was determined to understand and deal with those familiar feelings. Why did I feel such pride and honor but at the same time such pain, hurt, resentment, and anger. The emotions didn't seem to fit with one another. There had to be a reason why I felt as I did, and I was determined to figure it out.

Lying on my desk, in an old shoebox, was a stack of old letters that I had sent home to my mother while in Vietnam. She had recently returned them to me. I didn't know why I held onto them. I hadn't even read them since returning home. A photo album lay next to the box that was full of pictures that I had sent home. I remember Mom commenting that the pictures were always of me and my marine buddies sitting around in the jungle cooking our coffee over makeshift stoves made from C-ration cans burning heat tabs, a guy shaving, or some other meaningless domestic activity. I later explained to her that as soon as she sent me the disposable camera in the mail, I immediately took the pictures before the camera was ruined by the rain and that I didn't want the extra weight of the camera in my pack. Besides when you "hit the shit," the last thing on your mind was grabbing the camera to take pictures of a Viet Cong shooting at you. A marine always lightened the load he had to hump, even if it was a tiny camera. Also in the box was a yellow stained airline ticket, still neatly folded in its tattered cover. When I thought about the airline ticket, tears welled up in my eyes.

Staring at my son's picture I felt the all too familiar rage and anger swelling in my heart once again. I'd felt it for so many years, the burning desire to tell off America, to blast its politicians and citizens for what they had done to me and my fellow marines, and all the others who had served the country honorably, proudly, in battle. But I always kept my feelings about war to myself. I had tried so often to let the emotions go, but I never knew how. That's the tough part. Young minds are subjected to surreal situations and the only way to deal with them is to suppress them, which is the worst thing to do. For too many years I blamed myself for my bitterness and hostility but never understood why I felt that way.

Then, in my quiet office, watching it rain, I finally realized that the war was still a living part of me and had been for more than twenty-five years after coming home. My emotional war wounds were buried deep inside me, and even though dealing with them would be gut wrenching, if I ever hoped to find peace and release all of the heartache, fear and despair, loneliness, guilt, anger, bitterness, and every other emotion from my soul—let them drift away into the past and know that my war was over—I'd have to confront and deal with the pain and relive my entire experience of war. I would write it all down and then reread it a hundred times until I understood every word that flowed from deep within me. Maybe then I could sort out the truth about how I felt, and maybe others who I loved and cared about would be able to understand why I acted as I did when I returned home from Vietnam and would better understand what war was really like for a nineteen-year-old kid.

I rose from my chair and once again strolled over to the window. The rain was coming down hard, cascading from the roof and splashing on a banana tree in the flowerbed. Seeing the rain run off the leaves reminded me of the monsoon.

The monsoon crept in shrouded by dark, damp, dreary clouds. It was like living in a black-and-white photograph. The young faces of the marines grew sullen and their eyes blackened from not sleeping and they had a haggard, drawn look of despair, making their youthful faces seem much older. The thousand-yard stare of depression became etched on everyone's face. The stench of rotting skin on the marine's feet and the smell of soiled damp clothing mixed with gritty dirt clogging pores was still etched in my mind.

When the rain fell and the dark clouds hung low and the thunder rolled, I was reminded of the many lonesome days spent praying to God that the rain would stop. I'd get a fresh pair of dry socks, and he would let me survive just one more day.

I felt alone, stumbling through the darkness in Vietnam, searching for an answer that no one could give, like a story that had no end or a poem that made no sense. In such weather, I curled up in my poncho, wrapped tightly, lay on my side so only half of me got wet, and slept.

Winter soon drifted into spring then to summer, almost undetected. Only the calendar scratched on the side of every marine's helmet revealed which month it was and how many days he had left in country. Our skin, pale and white from months of being in the rain, soon turned red under the hot sun then a dark tan from months of exposure to the heat. At least being tan hid the dirt that accumulated on our skin from weeks of not bathing.

As I glanced down at the pictures in the album that lay opened on my desk, I realized that I was about to cry again. Sometimes when I was alone and thought about the war I would cry and never had a clue why. No one saw me do it. Marines don't cry; men don't cry. Why after so many years did the war affect me so? Why did I have such unexplained shame, guilt, and uncontrollable anger, violence that often came rushing out without warning? What were these emotions that I couldn't explain or understand? I felt like a walking time bomb ready to explode.

As I stood motionless, watching it rain, my breath fogged the window. The cold air of winter penetrated the glass and the tears came flowing from my eyes, rolling down my face like the rain sliding down on the windowpane. I began to sob and soon it turned to a loud, moaning cry, swelling from deep within. It was gut wrenching, as if I was about to vomit. I dropped to my knees and wrapped my arms around my chest and heaved back and forth. Never had I felt so distraught. For the first time since returning from my war, after twenty-five years, I finally, for some unknown reason, was letting my mournful soul scream and cry out, releasing my feelings, exploding them into the empty and darkening room without fear that someone could hear me. The outburst lasted only a few minutes, but for me it was as if decades of pain, sorrow, and heartache were being ripped from my guts.

I settled into my chair and closed my eyes, remembering.

Chapter 2

The tragedy of war is that it uses man's best to do man's worst.

—Henry Fosdick

It was a good day to join the marines. I rolled out of bed, threw on my jeans and a T-shirt, and took off to pick up Doug. He was actually waiting for me, which was a surprise. I was afraid that he might have changed his mind about joining. Doug was a cross between John Wayne and Charles Manson. He was six feet tall with a muscular build, black curly hair, ruddy complexion, and the darkest, meanest, and most haunting eyes you can imagine. He was your friend one minute and threatening to kick your ass the next. I figured he was the perfect guy to join the marines with. For some odd reason we got along well and he took care of me, like a little brother, since I was much smaller and a bit tamer than he was. But it didn't matter to me if he joined or not, because I was going into the marines anyway, with or without him.

I had cornered Doug the night before in our local hangout. He strolled into the place in typical fashion, sporting his usual jeans, motorcycle boots, T-shirt, and a black cowboy hat with a huge owl feather jutting out of a beaded Indian hatband. He neither owned a motorcycle nor liked Indians, but his wardrobe added to the eclectic personality of Doug. I decided that if I was joining the marines, he would be a perfect target for my sales pitch. All I need do was challenge him. I saw him bite the head off a lizard once for a dollar, so getting him to join the marines would be a snap.

"What's up, Doug?"

"Sideways, Dark," he grunted in his usual friendly way of saying hello.

"You know, it's been a real drag around here." I took a sip of beer. "I think it's time for me to do something with my life. Do something meaningful, go to new places and go where the action is." I tried to catch a reaction out of the corner of my eye, but he sat impassively.

"Let me buy you a beer, buddy." I poured his glass full. "Yep, I think I'm going to join the marines." Now I had his attention. He glanced at me from under his big-brimmed hat.

"I've got it all figured out. I'll sign up for two years, go to Vietnam, kick some ass, and then go to college on the G.I. Bill and let Uncle Sam pay the tab."

Doug stared at me. I thought either he was going to join me or he was getting ready to drink his beer, call me crazy, and laugh it off.

"Yeah, the way I see it, it really takes balls to join the marines. Some guys have guts and some don't." I finished my beer.

"Do you want to know what I think, Dark?" He stared at me intently. "I think you don't have the balls to join the marines. You know about as much about the marines as a hog knows about Christmas." That was an expression I'd not heard before. He continued. "I've got what it takes to be a marine. You wouldn't last a week. No balls, Dark. No balls, I say."

I had him. It was a done deal. I was trying to sell him on the idea and he was telling me no balls. We made our plans. I'd pick him up the next morning and we'd join on the buddy plan.

It was 1968, and I definitely needed a new plan for my life. I wrote a poem that summed it up.

Lost

> The path was dark as the wind blew across my face
> The moon cast shadows of the dancing leaves
> Upon the cold damp ground beneath my feet
> While the stripped bare branches moaned

As I walked on, there was no end in sight
Wandering aimlessly in the cold dark night
How long will I stroll down this desolate path
Before I become hopelessly lost forever

All alone and confused with nowhere to turn
Only the wind whispered to me softly
For there was nowhere to go
And sadly, no one was waiting

It was true: I had nowhere to go and no one was waiting. Yet there was a certain freedom to my situation as well. I had no responsibilities and no pressures to perform. College was out. I'd already blown that by flunking out of school due to skipping classes, and I wouldn't be able to avoid the draft. That was certain, and the thought never occurred to me anyway.

I had tried going to college at Miami Dade to become a hotshot pilot, but after rooming with five other guys who took the flying and partying more serious than the classes, I wasn't going to make it. My father actually called several of my instructors and asked if I had been going to class. One didn't even know who I was. Dad called one day to say that he had secured a position for me at the Doral Resort parking cars from 4:00 p.m. until midnight. I wasn't sure how I could go to class all day, fly in the afternoon, study, and then work until midnight, and eventually I'd had enough. I actually did obtain my private pilot's license and took the test to become a helicopter pilot in the army, but I deicide that wasn't my gig, so I packed my car and headed back home having dropped out of school, feeling like a failure.

Deep inside I wanted to serve America, and I thought joining the marines was the answer. The war in Vietnam was heating up big time, and one by one I saw my buddies getting drafted, so it was only a matter of time. It wouldn't take the Selective Service long to determine that I wasn't a college student any longer, which would make me 1-A for the draft—and I wasn't going into the army. My dad was a marine, and besides I'd heard that the marines were so bad that the Viet Cong thought twice about attacking them. No one I knew had been killed in Vietnam, and I thought that I was invincible, so why not? My plan had only one flaw. I had no idea what I was getting myself into. I suspect this is true for most young kids who join the service. We have these images of what a real soldier is and the honor of going into battle, having a real sense of pride and glory for country. The reality, however, can be very different.

But I needed to do something with my life, even if it was wrong. I had talked to several marines who were home on leave, and they said that I could join the marines for two years and once I served my tour in Vietnam I'd have only about six months left in the service and they'd probably give me an early out to go to college. It was that tour of Vietnam that I glossed over a bit too quickly. But I finally decided that I'd take that bold step toward being on my own, finally be a man and join the damned corps!

The year 1968 was a tumultuous time in America—race riots, political turmoil, Bobby Kennedy's and Martin Luther King's assassinations, and the peace movement clashing with the hawks for the war in Vietnam. Do we escalate the war or bring the troops home? Do we cut off the funding for the war? Big defense contractors were involved in scandals. For a kid of nineteen it was very confusing, and my parents were in the middle of a breakup, which made my life a little more difficult.

My father is Alvin Dark. I know it's been awhile and most won't remember who he is, but for most of his life he has been a major celebrity. He was without doubt one of the most talented athletes in the entire country for many years. My father was an All-American at LSU, lettering in football (as quarterback), baseball, basketball, and track. He was inducted into the LSU Hall of Fame, Louisiana Hall of Fame, and Oklahoma Hall of Fame. He was named Rookie of the Year of the National league in 1948 as a Boston Brave and later voted by the players to be Captain of the New York Giants, where he had his greatest years as a professional baseball player. He played and managed in five

World Series and was voted to the All-Star Game several times. His lifetime batting average was a respectable .289, and he had more than 2000 hits. He was an exceptionally devoted and dedicated athlete who would command millions in today's market, and had it not been for WWII and his stint in the marines, which took many years off his career, he would achieved much more.

In the famous clip shown hundreds of times on TV, he is number nineteen with the New York Giants jumping for joy around home plate after Bobby Thompson won the pennant in 1951 with his famous "shot heard round the world" home run against the Brooklyn Dodgers. My dad got things started that inning with a double. He later won the World Series as the shortstop in 1954 with the New York Giants. He went on to manage the 1962 Giants to a World Series, getting beat in the seventh game by the Yankees, and then won the 1974 World Series managing the Oakland Athletics when few critics gave them much of a chance to repeat as World Champions.

He never got along with the sports writers very well, so it's not hard to figure out why he hasn't been elected to the Baseball Hall of Fame. He actually has better stats than Reese or Rizzuto, who played shortstop for the Dodgers and Yankees respectively back in the heyday of the inner city New York rivalry. But that's a different story.

The important thing to note about my father is how he grew up poor, a son of a hardworking and honest oil-field driller from Oklahoma, who moved to Louisiana in the thirties. Dad survived the depression, Hitler, and the Japanese attack on Pearl Harbor, and he was a marine officer during the war. His only experience with war was to win at any cost, like everything else he did in his life. He always gave one hundred percent. Dad worked hard for everything he achieved. He had a paper route before school to earn his own spending money, and although he had natural athletic talent, it didn't come that easy to him because for an athlete he was small. I didn't realize it for many years, but he held the punting record at LSU for decades. I asked him once how he trained to become a great punter.

He said, "I placed a red flag on the ground in two locations about sixty yards apart and practiced kicking from one flag to the other for hours, trying to hit the flag with the punted ball. It was my idea of fun. Then when the game started, no matter what the situation was, I was prepared, and as a result I could place the opposing team deep in their own territory every time."

I also inquired what was it like to stand up to the plate back in the forties and fifties when baseball players didn't wear batting helmets and pitchers threw at ball players' heads routinely to intimidate a rookie player or to protect the inside of the plate. Where did he find the nerve to concentrate on hitting the ball instead of thinking about getting hit in the head by a one-hundred-mile-an-hour fastball?

Dad laughed and said, "I practiced getting out of the way."

I said, "Wait a minute. Explain that to me." I was trying to figure out how you practiced having a hard ball thrown at your head.

"Well," he said, "my older brother was a pitcher and we would get behind the house and practice. I'd stand up at the plate and he would throw a tennis ball to me. From time to time he would throw at my head, and I developed a unique move where I threw my feet directly out from under me, out over the plate, and fell straight backward to get out of the way." (I have actually seen a photo of him doing just that in a real game.) "Once I had the move perfected, my brother changed from the tennis ball to a hardball, and he would never let me know when he was going to throw at my head. Once I was confident that I could get out of the way of his fastball, I wasn't afraid anymore, and I never got hit in the head my entire big-league career."

Incredulous, I asked, "What about getting hit in the ribs, leg, or back? Didn't that scare you?"

He laughed again and said, "Getting hit in the ribs hurt, but it wasn't a career-ending event. It only hurt for a little while, and if I got hit that meant that I got on base, so there was no downside."

That, my friend, is a man I respect, a man who considered a hundred-mile-an-hour fastball in the ribs "taking one for the team." However, when it came to parental guidance when I needed advice, I got none. He wasn't the kind of dad who put up with excuses or thought much about anything except baseball or his other passion, golf. Had he done so, he couldn't have performed at the major league level. Kids did what they were told and didn't get in the way. He wasn't present when I was born because baseball season wasn't done yet. That was old school sports.

I once asked Dad what his backup plan was if he didn't make it to the big leagues. He answered with a surprised look, "I didn't have a backup plan. I always knew that I would play professional baseball."

I asked what he would have done if injured. He said, "Son, I did have an injury my entire career. I hurt my knee [which he had replaced a few years ago] while high jumping at a high school track meet in 1938. If I had opted for surgery back then, my career would have been over, so I just dealt with the pain."

I asked if his father ever sat down with him and discussed his future, such as what college he would attend or what his ambitions and goals were in life. "Oh no," he said, "that wasn't a subject that was ever discussed." His dad believed that a man just went to work—he worked hard and did the best that he could. His dad's only advice was that whatever he did in life, do a good job. If he washed cars, pretend that there was a sign on the side of the car that said "Washed by Alvin Dark." He also told him to always shine his shoes and brush his teeth and clean his fingernails. If a man's shoes weren't shined and his nails weren't clean, he could wear an expensive suit and still look bad.

That was it, all of a father's wisdom wrapped up in a few words. I was incredulous, and then it all made sense to me. My dad was a self-motivated man, and he couldn't understand why others weren't the same way. If you didn't achieve your goal, you didn't work hard enough. If your hands didn't bleed, you didn't take enough batting practice. If you didn't prepare, prepare, prepare, you would certainly fail. Life was that simple for him. It never dawned on him that perhaps his son was made a little differently and could have learned so much from his father's experiences. But those father-son talks never seemed to materialize. He wasn't a chatty guy.

So, right or wrong, I was taking charge of my life and into my inexperienced hands I placed my fate, making a decision about my future without even discussing the marines with my father. I'm not blaming him. I love and respect him. He is a great man and it was my choice to join the marines and go to war. I've dealt with my decision and it was mine alone.

The recruiter's office was on the third floor of the post office building downtown. When Doug and I stepped off the elevator, we both hesitated. What in the hell were we doing there?

Stalling, we found our way down the hall to the men's room and planned what we would say to the recruiter, then set off to his office.

As we approached the door, a deep voice blasted out, "Come on in, guys. Ready to join the corps?"

I was only five foot ten and weighed about 150 pounds. Suddenly I felt very inadequate standing next to impressive posters advertising the corps. Man, these marines were going to chew me up and spit me out. Getting over my intimidation, we told the marine we wanted to sign up on the buddy system, which meant that Doug and I would leave together and get assigned to the same unit.

The paperwork didn't take long to complete, since it was written so a third grader could fill in the blanks. We wouldn't leave for boot camp for a while, but as far as I was concerned I was already a marine! Once we signed the contract, I dropped off Doug at his house and headed home. I dreaded breaking the news to my parents. My dad was in town trying one more time to save the marriage, but things weren't going well, so there was a lot of tension in the house. What I had to tell them wasn't going to help matters. Mom had been very concerned about me being drafted. When I arrived home, my parents were both in their bedroom. I pushed open the door and sat down on the edge of the bed. Dad was preoccupied looking through his dresser drawer.

"Mom, Dad," I began nervously, "I've joined the Marine Corps today." Mom placed her arms around me and began to cry, then lashed out at my father as if it was his fault.

My father surprised me when he pointed his finger at me and said, "Son, don't ever ask me for another thing."

What an odd thing to say, I thought. Maybe I didn't understand his meaning. Had I asked him for anything? What did joining the marines have to do with asking him for anything? Anyway, I walked down the hall to my room and behind me I heard the argument start, and I regretted hurting them. But deep down I was excited and glad that I had taken control of my life and that I would soon be on my own. For a change, life was going to be exciting. The military has always been a haven for young, immature, confused kids who want to get away from home and start life on their own, and I was ready to go.

I finally got the call from the recruiter. We were leaving on December 30, 1968. Perfect, I thought, I'll be spending New Year's Eve in boot camp. For the first time, it dawned on me that I was really going to be a marine and go to Vietnam. Before signing up, I had occasionally listened to the news reports about Vietnam, watching the combat unfold on film, watching scenes of the marines living in the jungle and wounded marines being loaded on choppers, but now I turned up the volume and paid close attention. I suddenly realized how much I was going to miss my own bedroom, with my comfortable bed and my fan that squeaked just enough to lull and soothe me to sleep every night. I wasn't sure if I could sleep without the familiar sound of my fan in the background.

Until December 30 I vowed to sleep late every day, stuff myself with as many of my mom's homemade biscuits as possible, make myself sick eating pizza, and indulge myself in every way, making each pleasure last as long as possible. In this way the weeks passed quickly, and soon the time had come to leave.

Chapter 3

Your soul may belong to Jesus, but now your ass belongs to the Marine Corps.

—Sergeant Hartman, *Full Metal Jacket*

The recruiter called for us to come by his office and pick up our bus tickets. We were off to New Orleans. I never knew that I could be as lonesome as when I got on that bus and my family waved good-bye at the depot. At least I knew that once I completed my training I would be back home for thirty days of leave before going to Vietnam. Until then what I made of myself would be up to me, and I was going to give it a hundred percent. I was excited and scared to death, but I was determined not to show it.

I felt sorry for Doug. He had just received news that his girlfriend was pregnant. Hurriedly he got married in the courthouse with neither of the families even showing up. Both sets of parents didn't approve. Now Doug had a lot to think about, knowing that he was going to war with a wife and baby at home. I couldn't imagine that kind of pressure at his age.

Once arriving in New Orleans I checked into the LaSalle Hotel. It was just what I expected of the Marine Corps. It was an old, decrepit brick hotel with some of the letters missing from the neon sign. Inside, there sat an old guy wearing a three-day-old beard perched behind a stark counter, and a mail shelf was mounted on the wall behind him with the room keys lying inside. Each had a stick attached so no one would walk off with them. The lobby smelled of smoke and mold and dust.

marines wrapped in ponchos are hurriedly carried onto the bird by their buddies. The other marines load what appear to be body parts onto a third poncho and then hoist the hideous cargo aboard. Instantly, the chopper lifts off the ground, twisting the yellow smoke into a vortex and disappearing like a ghost. The noise from the fleeing choppers fades and the silence returns, as if nothing happened.

My heart races. I am helpless. I watch the remaining marines form into single file. Slowly they search the ground for more booby traps as they move out, cautiously and deliberately, into the dusk. The smaller squad of marines, having lost almost half their men, disappears into the evening and continues its patrol.

I wake up sweating.

Fifteen years went by. I saw a fellow marine who I served with in Vietnam, and as we talked I told him my dream. He looked at me, astonished, and said, "That happened, man. That was no dream. We were on road security. Don't you remember?"

It was bizarre to think that I had witnessed the tragedy yet didn't remember it. My terrified mind insulated me from the reality. It was my mind's way of protecting me yet leaving the memory behind in a more benign way, in the form of a dream lest I forget the horror of war.

For years after returning from war, it was hard to adjust to civilian life. Every time I saw a war-related broadcast or read a news article about the war, I felt guilty that I'd left my buddies on the battlefield. I carried the weight of war like the pack, ammo, and weapons I carried into battle. In reality, leaving the battlefield is only physical—you never really leave. Not a day goes by that I don't think of war. I will rarely talk about the war to anyone, but it's there, deep inside, and I know that talking about war to civilians who don't have a clue what I went through is a waste of time. The images are tightly woven into my dreams, reminding me of a distant life where the pale faces of my fellow marines no longer have names. Emotions still rule my life.

As I watch young soldiers being interviewed, sometimes it saddens me, because no one talks about the ugliness of battle. It's all balls to the

I checked in and went up the narrow stair to my room on the second floor. What a dump. I dropped on the bed, which surprisingly wasn't too bad, and looked out the window onto Canal Street, where things were bustling with activity as the partially lighted neon sign flashed red patterns on my wall. How was I going to sleep tonight? I missed my fan already.

It was a lonely evening. I didn't have much money. All of our possessions, our recruiter told us, would be sent home upon our arrival at boot camp, and he warned us not to carry cash in our pockets at boot camp. I decided to have a burger with my remaining cash and hang out in my room for the evening. Doug was supposed to get into town a little later, and I would meet him at the hotel.

As I lay stretched out on the bed I began to think about what the next years of my life would be like.

One of my favorite movies was *The 300 Spartans*, which was made in the early 1960s. In 480 BC, Xerxes, King of Persia, attacked Greece. The Spartans, the infamous warriors of Greece, who would be comparable to the modern day marines, were led by King Leonidas, who clashed with the Persians at the famed Pass at Thermopylae. There were only three hundred of them, outnumbered by a hundred to one, yet they held off the entire Persian army for days. In one scene, the Persian general confronts King Leonidas and tells him that unless he surrenders he will unleash his archers, who will fill the sky with arrows and blot out the sun.

Leonidas ponders his words for a few seconds and then defiantly stares at the general and says, "Then we will fight in the shade."

How brave Leonidas must have been. He refused to give up. He was eventually killed, and when he fell, the story goes, a great battle continued for four days over who would retain his body. The Spartans held off the Persians long enough for the rest of the Greek army to repel the enemy. This is the image I had of being a marine. I would lead a "Spartan" existence and try to gather courage to be tough, calloused, and unyielding.

Doug arrived later and together we managed to get to the Federal Building in downtown New Orleans the following morning. We got in line to take another physical and complete our paperwork. I realized that I would have to tolerate standing in lines. I'd taken a physical in Houston a month earlier, so this one was very brief, though interesting. I'd never stood in line with a hundred other naked guys who were bent over grabbing the ass cheeks with both hands while a doctor walked by quickly shining a flashlight up their butts. Evidently hemorrhoids were a big deal with the marines. What a site that had to be from the rear. A few probes and pokes and we were done. I suspected that at the height of the Vietnam War, when soldiers were desperately needed, that a deaf and blind spastic with one leg and a lisp could have passed the physical.

We stood with our right hand raised and promised to defend and serve our country, pledging our allegiance to the United States and to the Marine Corps. Duty, honor, country—I was a marine. At least I thought that I was. Because I was the only one with college under my belt, albeit a brief college stint, the duty sergeant assigned me the task of getting the "herd," as he called us, to our destination, Parris Island, South Carolina, the USMC Recruit Depot. Armed with a big manila envelope full of our orders, I loaded onto a bus with the others and we headed to the airport to catch our plane.

The atmosphere was charged with excitement and everyone was nervous, but we all tried to act tough. Clearly we all wondered what boot camp would really be like. One thing was certain: not every marine would be six feet tall and look like he was chiseled from granite. Most of these guys looked like a bunch of homeless bums the marines had found at a rehab center. My confidence was buoyed and I felt much better about my chances of making it knowing what my competition looked like. Just being in charge made me feel special.

We made it to the airport without incident. Once on board the plane, I leaned back in the seat and closed my eyes, reflecting on my life. Objectively, I thought that I was a pretty boring and simple guy who was basically a good person. I'd been picked up by the cops only once in high school (for stealing Coke bottles during a gag that went very wrong), but no charges were filed. I never did drugs even though I had plenty of opportunities, and I never could hold my liquor, so I wasn't much of a drinker or party type. I did go on a hitchhiking adventure with Doug and another buddy while waiting to go into the corps, but even that had been uneventful. Our destination was California but we ended up in Mississippi—but it would take awhile to explain how we ended up there. We slept in the woods for a few days before we had enough of that adventure and caught a bus home. This experience of joining the corps would be by far the most adventurous time of my life, and the big question that I had was: Could I measure up? Would I be able to "take it"? One thing was certain: I wasn't going to fail. It was my biggest fear—failure. It just wasn't an option.

I drifted off to an uncomfortable half sleep, and when I heard, "Please raise your seats to an upright position for landing," my stomach started flipping.

Man, what had I gotten myself into? I had to be crazy. I could be at home right now enjoying my freedom, but no, I'd actually joined the Marine Corps. I'd never make it. What was I thinking? Filled with doubt, I deplaned, ready to face the next ten weeks of certain hell.

Once we unloaded and gathered at the terminal lobby, one of the guys said he needed to visit the restroom. While he went inside to do his thing, a very large guy dressed in marine fatigues approached us.

In a booming voice he said, "Which one of you idiots is in charge?"

"I am, Sarge," I reluctantly said, not too sure why a guy I didn't even know was calling me an idiot. I held out the big envelope with our orders in it, which I had guarded since receiving it in New Orleans.

He grabbed it. "I'm not a sergeant, you dumb shit. Just give me the envelope and get in line with the rest of the shitheads. Is everyone present and accounted for?"

"Everyone except a guy who needed to take a dump," I said, less sure of myself this time.

"All right, all of you ladies get in line against the wall and shut up." He turned and headed into the restroom where we heard loud cussing and a door slam, and out rolled the guy who was using the restroom, hurriedly zipping up his jeans.

"That man is nuts," the guy mumbled, still struggling with his zipper and speaking in a whisper so the marine couldn't hear him, "Man, he jumps in my stall and yells, 'Pinch it off, dickhead, and get your ass in line!'"

I was still trying not to laugh when we all herded onto the bus, where the marine stood in the aisle.

"I don't want to hear one swinging dick say nothing. If I hear a peep, you will pay. Do you pricks hear me?"

We all kind of mumbled yeah, okay, a few yes sirs, and then things got real quiet. Marine life was going to be interesting.

As we pulled into the base, a big red sign divided the road with US Marine Corps Recruit Depot, Parris Island, South Carolina, written on the plaster face of the sign. Once inside the gate, I saw a huge asphalt paved area that must have been ten acres or larger, and even though it was growing dark, groups of marines were running in unison, singing in rhythm, being lead by a marine carrying a red banner with a yellow number on it and a drill instructor screaming at them. Before our bus even stopped, the door flew open and a mean-ass blond marine, about five foot seven inches tall and well over two hundred pounds of pure muscle, leaped into the aisle.

"You will get your asses off this bus and place your feet on the painted footprints on the pavement outside, now, now, now!"

We all jumped for the aisle at the same time, throwing guys left and right, and before ten guys were able to get off the bus, the same drill instructor was yelling to get back on the bus because we weren't moving fast enough.

"Get your asses back on the bus you bunch of slow-moving pussies. We can play games all night long if you want to play grab-ass with me. Now get off this bus you bunch of retards."

Off we went again, this time everyone ending up on the footprints on the pavement. Now several other DIs—as the drill instructors were called—began running through the ranks thrusting the brims of their perfectly formed DI hats into the bridge of our noses as they yelled in our faces, spitting on purpose as they screamed out our orders.

"You bunch of dirtbag recruits will keep your pieholes shut, eyes to the front, and do what you are told. Stand at attention, do exactly as I say, and whatever I tell you to do, you turn to it fast—and I mean fast—or we'll do it all night. You will carry out my orders without questions, and recruits do not speak until they are spoken to. The first and last thing out of a recruit's mouth is sir! Do you understand?"

In unison we hollered, "Sir, yes sir."

"What do I have here, a bunch of queers? I can't hear you."

This time we yelled at the top of our lungs, "Sir, yes sir."

Still not satisfied, he screamed, "I can't hear you, faggots."

This time we answered we must have satisfied him, because he told us to turn to the right and get our asses in line as we faced a green metal building. We herded in the door, and as the line shortened I saw what was happening to the guys in front. In about thirty seconds, the barbers shaved each man's head slicker than a bowling ball. As we marched into the next room, we passed a mirror with "Welcome to the Marine Corps" stenciled on it. There I stood looking at myself with my cleanly shaven white-skinned head where blond locks used to be, and for the first time in my life I actually looked mean, like a convict. I could have been on a FBI poster.

We were herded into one line after the other, getting our shots in both arms at the same time, picking up various items, socks, "skivvies," trousers, caps, boots, and other assorted gear. Everything we wore to the base and everything we had in our pockets was boxed up and sent home to "Mommy," as the DIs instructed. Since it was approaching midnight by the time we packed our gear, we stuffed everything into a seabag (a duffel bag). Because we didn't know how to march yet the DI insisted that we all moo like cows as the herd moved across the large asphalt parade deck to our barracks, which would be home for the next ten weeks. The entire distance, DIs were screaming and pushing us, many recruits falling down and getting run over by the ones behind them. Midnight must have been close, and it dawned on me that it would be New Year any minute and that this was the worst possible place to celebrate.

Our barracks was a two-story wood-framed rectangular building. When we filed into the first floor I was greatly relieved, since we wouldn't have to run up and down the stairs a hundred times because we didn't get there fast enough. Once inside, our beds (or racks, as they called them) were lined next to each other two rows on one side of the room and two more on the other. They were steel bunk beds with a very thin mattress over a wire mesh spring. There was no way this bed would be comfortable, but that was the least of my worries.

"Get your ass in front of a rack you bunch of pussies," the DI screamed as we briefly played musical chairs for a bunk then struggled to come to a form of attention. Three DIs were walking up and down the ranks, and we got very quiet.

"I am Gunnery Sergeant Marx. I am the senior drill instructor for First Battalion Platoon 101." Gunny was a very small marine, maybe five foot six inches tall and 140 pounds, but he was "squared away," nothing out of place and had a huge deep voice which I'm sure took practice to obtain. He also had dark, piercing eyes. I respected him immediately. He looked tough and I could tell he was a seasoned marine.

"This is Assistant Drill Instructor Sergeant David," he said as he pointed to a stocky marine that I remembered from the bus incident, the guy who liked running us off and on the bus time after time. Sergeant David was a stereotypical marine. He was blonde but cut his hair "high and tight." A solid six feet and over two hundred pounds, standing with his chest out and his arms folded behind him, he was very impressive.

"This is Assistant Drill Instructor Staff Sergeant Austin." I thought this man looked exactly like Bill Cosby.

I thought that any minute now we would settle into our bunks and finally get some rest. I'd been up for almost twenty-four hours and was exhausted, but to my dismay "Gunny," as Gunnery Sergeant was referred to by the other DIs, yelled, "Jumping jacks. Ready begin: one, two, one, two … faster, faster, faster … down on your bellies, get up, get up." Some of the men were still doing jumping jacks and others were dropping to the deck and trying to bounce up again as Gunny shouted out his orders.

"Oh my God, what have I got here? You bunch of faggots want to be marines? Get your asses down on the deck. Get up, get up!"

We played this game until guys were dropping out, coughing and nearly fainting from exhaustion, but the night was just getting started. They wanted to show us how we should run in and out of the barracks, so, just for practice, we ran out of the barracks and learned how to get into formation. Then we ran inside to stand at attention in front of our racks. We were always at attention. We did that about ten times, once again running over the ones who tripped or were shoved to the ground by the DI.

Finally, and mercifully, Gunny Marx shouted to take off our boots, tie the laces together, drape them around our necks, get into our racks, come to a position of attention, and sleep. Periodically, a marine who was walking "fire watch," as the marines called it, would shine a flash light in your face and yell at you, "Are you asleep!" and of course you were supposed to answer yes or no. If it was Sir, no sir, then you were in trouble for not sleeping thus not obeying your orders, so you did pushups, and if you answered Sir, yes sir, then you were accused of talking in your sleep, which meant you had to get out of bed and do pushups for speaking without permission. Obviously, no one could sleep with all the shouting going on, which was their plan: to break us the first night. They did a good job.

As soon as I closed my eyes and drifted off to an uneasy sleep for what seemed to be ten minutes, a trash can came flying into the room and the lights came on while the DIs roamed up and down the ranks shouting at us demanding that we mop the floors, take out the garbage cans (even though there wasn't any trash in them yet), and make up our bunks (which we hadn't been allowed to sleep in yet), so that didn't take long. It couldn't have been later than 4:30 in the morning. Everyone was spent.

I learned a very valuable lesson on my very first morning of boot camp: the guy who could grab the trash can first and run outside to empty it into the dumpster could, in the shadows and cover of darkness, take a long and comfortable piss. That was a huge discovery. When I returned from dumping the garbage, of which there was none, until the barracks was "squared away," as the DI said, no one took a leak (or, as the marines said, "made a head call"). Guys were squirming and holding their crotch desperately needing to take a whiz while I remained calm and comfortable. The lesson I learned was if you are faster and outthink your buddy, you might just do well in the marines. I was determined to be first to wake in the morning and leap for the trash can. I'd fight for that trash can if need be. However, if you got caught taking a leak by the dumpster you would be in big trouble, but I never got caught.

Of course, we had to run in and out of the barracks a dozen times until we did it right, but we were finally off to the, "chow hall," a place every marine would grow to love. The first morning was a memorable experience, but for all of the wrong reasons. We were told to get into the line at chow so close to the guy in front of us that we were literally smashed between one another. From the lack of sleep and no chow, with a touch of constipation from not having my morning quiet time alone on the john, I passed out for a few seconds. I never hit the ground but got carried along with the flow of marine recruits trying to get fed. Once in the chow line, you held out your tray when you wanted the food item and they threw the chow on to your tray. Of course, whatever went on your tray was what you ate, all of it—I mean every bite. And just to make sure it was all gone, a DI stood at the trash can where you raked your tray clean, and you better not have been throwing any chow away.

I was sitting next to a guy named Magee who obviously wasn't feeling well when all of a sudden he threw up on his tray. He had turned ghostly white. He staggered over to the trash can to dump the vomit and food into the trash and, to my horror and his, the DI said, "Sit your dumb ass down and eat every bite. No one wastes my Marine Corps chow." I watched as Magee sat down and took a bite, which almost made me hurl, and then he threw up again. The DI screamed at him, grabbed him by the shirt, and dragged him out the door, and from that day until boot camp graduation, Magee was known as Private Puke. We were allowed only five minutes to eat, and once we passed the tray inspection we fell into formation outside of the chow hall then headed back to the barracks for more fun and games.

We ran in and out of the "barn," as Gunny called it several more times for good measure and then stood in front of our racks and were introduced to squat thrusts, more jumping jacks, and of course push-ups until we turned blue.

Staff Sergeant Austin shouted out the commands while Gunny and Sgt. David roamed up and down the ranks making sure that everyone was giving a hundred percent effort.

Sgt. David had a Brooklyn accent, calling us, "Yous guys," which was irritating to listen to, and SSgt. Austin was the comedian of the group. He would begin exercises, or "PT" as he called it, by yelling, "Ladies, jumping jacks, ready begin, forever," which I hated, since you didn't know how many reps he was going to make you perform.

Once we finished, we stood at attention as the three DIs started closely inspecting us, evaluating the "herd." Staff Sergeant Austin stopped in front of my rack and began to circle my bunkmate, Private Skorupa. He had to be at least six foot six and couldn't have weighed more than 175 pounds, and he had the kind of face and build that a DI just couldn't pass up. I hadn't noticed, but when Skorupa had his head shaved they left a tuft of hair on the side of his head, which stood out prominently when the rest of his was so clean shaven. SSgt. Austin was fascinated with the clump of hair.

He reached up, poked it, pulled on it a few times, got that smirk on his face, and looked up to Skorupa and said, "Hey, you Ichabod Crane–looking idiot, what damned planet are you from?"

I thought I would die trying not to laugh, but I held it in.

"Hey, Gunny, come look at this. I think we have us an alien from outer space. You deaf, yo-yo? I asked your dumb ass what planet are you from?"

Poor Skorupa looked at him, making eye contact, which was a mistake because it was forbidden to look into the eyes of a DI, and said, "Earth, sir."

Now Gunny was on top of him shouting at him that he was trying to be a hippie and grow his hair long in the Marine Corps, and where did he get off "eye-balling" him? Old Skorupa didn't know what to do, and every time he answered it was the wrong response, so he dropped down and began doing pushups "forever," while I had to stand there right next to him and not laugh. I thought this show could go on Broadway and be a big hit.

Mercifully, Gunny moved on to his next target. I sighed in relief when Gunny didn't find anything wrong with me.

"Ladies, I'm going to be your mama for the next ten weeks," Gunny said as he suddenly wheeled around in the aisle to see if he could catch anyone off guard, not paying attention.

"You are a bunch of dirtbags. You are slime. You are nothing but maggots. But my beloved corps tells me that I have to make marines out of you, and by God, I will, even if it kills you in the process. Now listen up, dirtbags. Recruits address me as sir and only sir. Recruits will not address me as 'you.' A ewe is a female sheep, and I ain't no female sheep. I know what you farm boys do to sheep, and when you call me a ewe that means that you want to screw me too ... and you ain't screwing me." He crossed his hands behind his back, had his chest puffed out, and slowly walked down the middle of the squad bay choosing his words carefully.

"Do you maggots hear me?" Gunny stared.

"Sir, yes sir," we screamed.

His dark eyes glared at us from beneath the brim of his hat as he strolled past us, taking his time. "Everything is done quickly in my beloved corps. A slow marine is a dead marine. I want one hundred percent for my beloved corps, and if I don't get one hundred percent for my beloved corps, everyone pays. If any of you sissy bastards quit, you all pay. Jumping jacks. Ready, begin." Gunny watched closely to see who was slacking off or giving up, and man did they pay.

Finally, after what seemed like hours, we were told to come to a position of attention and it was time for us to learn how to come to the position correctly. The way the marines teach the position of attention is interesting. The fatigues we were wearing were pretty baggy, so when the DI thought that you were not standing erect enough, the DI would grab your shirt, make a fist, pull your shirt out, and ram his fist in your stomach just below your sternum. Your breath left you, and his thrusting, powerful blow almost made you pass out. This wasn't beating a recruit; it was correcting your position of attention.

Gunny went on to teach us about the Marine Corps way of bathing, shaving, talking, sleeping, and every other aspect of our lives, which would be totally controlled by our DI from now on. Everything was by the book. Our footlocker was arranged perfectly, with the socks folded next to the skivvies, trousers next to the extra pair of boots, which was next to the soap, and so on. Everyone's gear had to be aligned exactly the same, and if it wasn't, you paid, everyone paid.

I had gone into the marines with the intention of excelling, of showing the corps what a guy from Louisiana could do. Now I changed my mind and decided to lay low and not attract attention. We eventually fell into a routine and the first two weeks flew by. After getting a few good nights of sleep, I began gaining strength from the PT and good food. I actually started feeling better. We were so busy that I actually hadn't even talked with Doug to see how he was doing. He was in a different squad, and since there was no talking, we didn't. Occasionally our eyes met and we cracked a thin smile at each other. I could read his mind.

In the next few days we started classes, learning about the differences between ranks and about the chain of command all the way from our assistant DI to the President of the United States. Every night we would stand on our footlockers and recite every superior officer's name and rank until we could repeat them without thinking.

We picked up the remainder of our gear, including our rifles, packs, canteens, and other infantry-related equipment, and were instructed on how to store it. Our rifles were to be strapped to our rack in a precise position. We were vaccinated and told how to brush our teeth, clean our ears, and care for our skin. It was clear that some of the recruits were learning about personal hygiene for the first time. Guys were sent to the dentist for rotten teeth, or to sick bay (base hospital) for sores in their scalp, and if the recruit was very overweight he was sent to the Fat Body Platoon. There the overweight recruit lived on eggs and lettuce and PT'd until they lost the weight; then they rejoined our platoon. They often looked so different that we didn't recognize them. I could imagine what their parents would think when they saw them at graduation in a few months.

We stayed so busy that I didn't have much time to miss home, until the lights went out. Then I missed my bed, the bathtub, my own private toilet, and my mom's home cooking. But as soon as my head hit the pillow I was sound asleep.

One night after the lights went out one private got up and fled down the middle of the squad bay, hit the screen door at a dead run, and raced out of the barracks. Apparently he had cracked under the pressure.

The next morning Gunny was livid. He threw on the lights and screamed, "Attention," with more emotion in his voice than normal.

We fell out in front of our racks at attention. "Quitting is a sign of weakness, and I'm going to make you pussies pay." I couldn't quite figure out how it was fair to make us pay, since I didn't even know the guy and had nothing to do with his decision to haul ass, but the marines aren't about being fair. Gunny raved on. "I'm going to teach you what it means to be a team, a fighting unit! No one quits. If one guy gives up or falls out on a march, someone else has to carry his load. Only when you have learned to work as a unit, brother to brother, marine to marine, can you ever defeat the enemy."

In one leap he jumped on top of the table in the middle of the squad bay, and with his dark black eyes glaring at us, his jaw sticking out and his face red with rage as the veins in his neck bulged out, he continued his tirade.

"You ladies are going to Vietnam. Do you think you are going to a church picnic? I've been to Nam, and it's no picnic. I've seen my fellow marines with their guts hanging out, and I had to stuff them back in. I've watched men die, twisting in pain as they held my hand screaming at me to let them die. I've smelled the rotting flesh of the enemy on the battlefield with his brains drying out in the sun. I've humped through the jungles and paddies of Nam, thirsty beyond belief, dropping down, brushing away the scum and drinking the foul water while the sun beat down on my back like a two-ton weight. You pussies won't last one minute in Nam unless you learn to work together and never, never, ever quit."

We were mesmerized by his every word, riveted by the intensity of his voice, and we were beginning to realize that our DIs were here to teach us and prepare us for battle. I sensed the tremendous burden he carried, knowing that his recruits were going to face the same nightmares in Vietnam that he still dealt with every night. He had to teach us to survive, just as his DI had taught him years before. Silence filled the barracks as he went on.

"You can never give up, never quit! There's always that ten percent, the shitbirds who keep the other ninety percent pissed off because they get the good marines killed. I won't have shitbirds in Platoon 101, do you hear me?"

"Sir, yes sir," we all screamed in unison.

"Pride, ladies, pride in the corps! There is no greater honor than killing the enemy while Johnny sits at home porking your girlfriend, little Mary Rotten Crotch. You better forget her, because she has already forgotten you. You'd better think about killing the enemy, because I can assure you that he can't wait to kill you. Marines don't die for their country. That's bullshit. We let those little slopeheaded bastards die for their piece-of-shit country. We kill the enemy, and they're scared shitless of us, and do you know why?"

He paused and looked around the still barracks. "Because we are *Marines!* Ah-ooh-gaah!" Gunny roared as he leaped from the table. He ran up and down the barracks and bellowed, "Marine Corps! All good! Marine Corps. All good! Shout it out, ladies!"

We shouted at the top of our lungs and became more fired up with every chorus we screamed.

"Yes, ladies," Gunny said, his eyes glittering, "we kill those little bastards, those son of a bitches, before they even know what hit 'em. Those little gooks lie awake at night scared shitless that a marine is gonna cut him wide-ass open and pull his guts out, laughing in his face the entire time." He scowled. "But you pussies aren't marines. You want to go home to Mommy, don't you?"

"Sir, no sir," we yelled, working ourselves into a frenzy.

Gunny got a little calmer now. "Well, do me a favor. If you decide to run away, or to kill yourself, at least do a good, clean job of it. If you are gonna cut your wrist, don't do it in your rack. Go stand in the shower so we can flush your no good chicken-shit blood down the drain! Will you do that for me?"

"Sir, yes sir," we shouted, not sure what we were agreeing with.

"When I get through with you pricks, you are going to be the meanest sons of bitches that ever marched out of Parris Island. Now fall out, assholes."

As he turned his back to us, we all dived madly for the door, skirting him carefully so as not to touch him. And for the first time since arriving at boot camp, we only had to run out of the barracks once. For the first time, I felt a sense of pride developing, a feeling that we were different today, that we were becoming marines.

Chapter 4

Some people live an entire lifetime and wonder if they have made a difference in the world, but the marines don't have that problem.

—President Ronald Reagan

"Are you a mean son of a bitch, Private?" Gunny asked me that night as I stood in front of my rack.

"Sir, yes sir!"

"To me you look like a big pussy." His voice was sarcastically soft and feminine. "Are you a queer?"

"Sir, no sir." I used the deepest voice I could muster.

"Well, we'll see about that, dirtbag. You better not screw up. I'll be watching you closely. Get your ass down to the first bunk. You are squad leader of First Squad. Move it. Move it before I change my mind."

I moved my gear so quickly that the other guy currently occupying the rack wasn't moved out before I was standing tall in front of my new home. I and the other three squad leaders stood at attention in the center of the squad bay.

"Now I want the meanest bastard in Platoon 101 to step out," Gunny yelled.

Doug and a few others stepped out to accept the challenge, but Doug was by far the most intimidating private in the platoon. With his head shaved, his ruddy complexion, and those crazy eyes, he looked like a Hell's Angel. After the usual insults, Doug was selected platoon guide. He would carry the Platoon 101 banner and lead the Platoon wherever we went. Not until later did we learn that in reality he was the DI's thug who did his dirty work for him when a recruit needed a little attention. I knew that if anyone screwed up, they would pay. When Gunny handed the banner to Doug, he said that until we showed him we wanted to be marines, the banner would remain rolled up around the pole. Not until we proved ourselves would he allow it to be unfurled.

After our selection, Gunny called us into his room, or house as he called it. This was a real honor, because normally a recruit wasn't even allowed to look into the doorway of his house. He made us drop to our knees at attention, I suspect because this allowed him to look down at us from his height. He lectured us about what it meant to be a leader and how he was counting on us to set an example. As he spoke, he fondled his .45-caliber pistol, rubbing it with an oiled cloth. We would be held to a higher standard and accountable for everything that our squad did. If anyone in our squad screwed up, we would pay. I started to doubt my enthusiasm for becoming a squad leader, but I knew that things would be different now and I'd better get with the program and give one hundred percent. My men would have to do their part as well, because I wasn't going to pay for their screwups.

After lights went out, Doug called a meeting of the squad leaders to discuss how we could enhance our performance. We decided that when the lights went out, the platoon would dress quietly, make up our racks, and sleep on top of our bedding so in the morning we could finish our chores quickly. Sleeping in uniform violated marine rules, but we knew the DIs would look the other way, because when the lights went on everything would be squared away and we would be standing tall in front of our racks, ready to start our day.

The next morning I had my first taste of leadership when one of my guys had his pillow turned the wrong way and of course Gunny caught the mistake. Instead of the recruit who had screwed up, I dropped down to do fifty pushups. Later, when Gunny wasn't looking, I punched the guy in the gut and told him to get his act together. If I had to pay, he would too.

As a platoon, we were getting stronger from running and other physical training we did every day. But some guys had a hard time. One day after a tough run during which several guys couldn't keep up fell out and started walking, life became hell. When we got back to the barn, we lined up and all three DIs started racing up and down the ranks, shoving and cussing us, and we began to pay with squat-thrusts forever. This exercise period had a very sadistic tone, and I knew it was going to be excruciating.

"Okay, quitters, front and center!" he yelled, running around the ranks and hurling the guys who had quit on the run to the floor at the center of the squad bay.

It was obvious that those who had quit were scared shitless as they lay on the floor in the position of attention, all lined up close to each other. Then Gunny ripped a sheet off one of the racks and covered the quitters. Then he ordered the rest of the platoon to file by "the dead," as he referred to them, and kick them as we passed, calling them "quitters."

"You see these dead marines," yelled Gunny. "These marines are dead because they quit. Charlie wants you to quit. He needs you to quit. Charlie is waiting for you to fall out of a hump so he can slip up on your dumb ass and cut your throat. Do you think you can whip Charlie if you quit? He humps night and day for weeks on end just to carry a bag of rice to his buddies. He doesn't know the word quit. He is a tough little bastard who will never give up. If you quit, then you die and other good marines die. Do you understand?"

We all screamed a unified, "Sir, yes sir!"

He turned to the squad leaders and said, "Squad leaders, front and center." We scrambled to the center of the squad bay.

"No more quitters. If anyone falls out of another run, you ladies are going to pay. Your ass will belong to me, and you will wish that you were dead. Is that clear, you bunch of dickheads?"

"Sir, yes sir," we screamed, and we were pissed as well. The men knew exactly what the new rules would be. If we had to pay, then they had to pay. No one had better fall out of another run.

◆   ◆   ◆

Even though boot camp was deadly serious ninety percent of the time, the other ten percent was often hilarious. Once, Gunny selected the smallest marine in the platoon, Private Beaman, and yelled, "Beaman, front and center."

Beaman was about five feet two inches tall and couldn't have weighed more than 120 pounds. Beaman hustled down to the center of the squad bay and came to attention, snapping his boot heels together, and in a high-pitched voice screamed, "Sir, Private Beaman reporting as ordered, sir!"

"Okay, you little prick, from now on you are Private House Mouse."

Beaman stood erect and frozen, not sure what a house mouse did, but I had it figured out. The house mouse ran errands, got the DIs coffee for him, picked up the mail, and basically did anything Gunny wanted him to do.

"Are you a mean little mouse?" Gunny asked Beaman. "Because I don't want no pussy for a house mouse. I want a mean little bastard. Sometimes we have house-mouse fights between platoons, and my mouse better be tough. I bet you're a nasty-ass marine!"

"Sir, yes sir," Beaman screamed once again. I wanted to laugh so bad but held in the laughter, knowing that I'd get my "position of attention corrected."

"Okay, you wicked little bastard, I want you to go up stairs to Platoon 102 and you walk up to that ignorant, dumbass drill instructor on duty and you tell him that you are the meanest son of a bitch on Parris Island, and to prove it you are going to kick his ass." Mouse was horrified and didn't know what to think. He stood frozen.

Gunny screamed in his face, "Get your ass upstairs, and don't wimp out on me, either, or you will pay!"

We heard Mouse run up the stairs and all was quiet. Then we heard him running down the stairs, and when he returned he ran into the squad bay and pulled up to attention in front of Gunny. His pants, hat, belt, and shirt were on backward, and his boots were tied together by the shoe laces and wrapped around his neck. Mouse had a tiny smile on his face and he was desperately trying not to laugh.

"Mouse, did you kick that drill instructor's ass?" Gunny was trying not to laugh as well.

By now we were all grunting and snorting, and Gunny could hear us, but it was time to enjoy a light moment.

Mouse screamed out, "Sir, yes sir."

Gunny smirked and said, "You lying turd. Turn your gear around and clean your damned rifle. Tough my ass. You couldn't whip my mother."

◆   ◆   ◆

Every night while preparing to shower, we stood at attention on our footlockers—dressed in our boxers, T-shirt, and flip-flops, our shaving gear in one hand and our belt in the other. We had to scrub our belt clean every time we took a shower. Perched on our footlockers one evening, I noticed that the guy directly across from me had started to grab his crotch and squirm. I could tell that he needed to take a leak bad, but under no circumstances would you ask the DI for permission to make a head call right before showering. The longer we stood there the more he shook. I could hardly keep a straight face. Finally, not being able to hold it any longer, he turned around and started to piss on the bunk behind him. The guy standing on his foot locker next to him was horrified because it was his rack the guy was pissing on. We couldn't hold it in any longer, and loud laughter broke out. Sgt. David was on duty, and when he heard the laughing he came running down to our end of the barn, grabbed the private by the throat, and hurled him on to the rack, making him roll around in the piss. He then had to wear his piss-stinking clothes for a few days and sleep in the rack with the smelly sheets until even Sgt. David couldn't stand him anymore.

◆   ◆   ◆

I developed a horribly painful earache about four weeks into boot camp. As I lay in my rack one night, I was rolling and twisting, pulling at my ear in excruciating pain. I knew if I went and woke up Gunny and requested to go to sickbay to see the doc, he'd probably never let me live it down. So instead I just lay there in agony. Then suddenly I felt my ear explode as fluid ran down the side of my face. It was actually a great relief since the pressure was gone, but I couldn't hear anything with my right ear, just a ringing sound. I rubbed the side of my head and even in the dim light coming through the window I could tell that I had blood pouring out of my ear and it was ringing inside my head. I was scared of what Gunny would do if I asked to report to sickbay, but hell—I couldn't hear a thing and figured that I had no choice.

There was a specific way to knock on a DI's door. The recruit had to stand at attention with his left shoulder against the door trim, reach over with his right hand, and knock on the door, all the while looking straight ahead. You never looked gunny in the eye or turned your head. In this position, a recruit could not look into the DI's "house," as he called it. I approached with much trepidation, took my position at the door, and boldly knocked. The door flew open and in a flash Gunny jumped in my face, standing in his skivvies.

"Private Dark, what in the hell do you want, maggot? It's midnight, dipshit." Gunny couldn't see the blood smeared on my face because my left shoulder was against the door trim and my right ear was turned away from him.

"Sir, the private requests permission to go to sickbay, sir." I rotated so Gunny could see the blood on my face. When he saw it he jumped back a foot or two and screamed.

"Holy shit, private. Permission granted, and you better not tell him that I did this to you." I might have known that his only concern was not getting in trouble for beating a private.

I reported to sickbay and the doc on duty gave me some antibiotics and some wonderful pain medication. I crawled in a rack and crashed. For the first time at boot camp, I slept like a log. The next morning the doc on duty came by and said that it would be a week or two before I could go back to the field, and then I'd be assigned to another platoon. I was devastated. They called guys who joined another platoon a "pickup," and they caught all the worst crap from the DIs. DIs figured if you were a "pickup," you were a quitter. I told the Doc I had to go back to my platoon. I was fine, I said. I had no pain and was ready to report. He held up his watch to my ear.

"Can you hear the ticking?"

"Yes sir!" I said confidently. He knew I was lying but I guess he figured that if I was nutty enough to want to rejoin the platoon, he'd let me go. He loaded me up with antibiotics and let me return to the platoon. Of course, I had to get on my knees and beg Gunny to have me back, but I could tell he wanted me. After all, I'd proven myself as a squad leader and he knew I wasn't a quitter.

◆　　◆　　◆

The more Gunny preached to us the more we respected him. All of our DIs had been to Nam and we saw them as heroes. If any one of them had told us to run through a wall, we would have given it a hundred percent effort. They became like our fathers, and everyone wanted to please them.

We didn't realize it at the time, but were we being trained not only physically for the harshness of war but also mentally. We were being brainwashed to fight and kill on the battlefield. This was necessary because of the job that we were going to have to do in Vietnam. It was a simple formula: they broke us, motivated us, and molded us into a unit. We had no TV, no newspapers, no voice contact with the outside world, no phone calls home, only an occasional letter. The marines isolated us from everything going on in the world so they could twist and shape our innocent minds into that of a soldier who would follow orders without hesitation. They convinced us that even though only a few weeks ago we had showed up at Parris Island as a bunch of undisciplined individuals, now, after a few short weeks, we had been transformed magically into marines. We were invincible. We had become a fighting unit. We could not be beaten by the enemy.

The DIs filled us with the pride of being a marine, and serving our country was now the most glorious thing that an American could do. If cast onto the battlefield, we would fight to the death. This was the marines' mission, to make us killers, and we were ready to be molded.

All I knew was that my body was changing, my mind was being toughened, I was more disciplined, and I had a sense of confidence deep inside me for the first time in my life. I was on my own and I was holding up. I learned what it was like to be a leader, and although I had to pay when one of my men screwed up, it still felt good be in a position of authority. I was excelling at a very difficult task and handling everything that this tough-assed DI could throw at me, and I felt good about myself. I could do this. I would not fail. I was becoming a man.

Boot camp could be ridiculous as well. Guys were made to piss in their pants when the Gunny refused to let them make a "head call," or if he wanted to have real fun he'd let him go but ordered him to imitate the sound of an emergency siren as he ran to the head. The DI played games at mail call by holding out a letter for you and just when you reached for it moving it so you stood there trying to grab your letter while remaining at attention.

If they hated you and felt that you should perform better, they could always send you to Motivation Platoon for a day or two, and that's all it usually took to get a guy "motivated." Once, a guy in our platoon was found with a few bucks in his pocket, so to make an example of him they sent him to Motivation Platoon. It was nothing more than a PT platoon, running guys until they dropped or marching them through the swamp that surrounded Parris Island in full gear until the mud covered them so thick that they were unrecognizable.

Then there was the Psychiatric Platoon, which was reserved for guys who were really nuts or tried to act like it to get out of the marines. We had a guy who while standing fire watch, gathered everyone's canteens and piled them under his rack. The next morning he failed to wake up the Gunny at the appropriate time, and when Gunny saw all the canteens stored under his rack, it was off to the Psych Platoon for that guy.

The longer we were in boot camp the more tolerable it became. The DIs became predictable and we knew what pushed their buttons. Once we got rid of the shitbird guys who couldn't cut it, were injured, or broke mentally we worked together like a true team. We didn't have to "pay" as often, and things were clicking. We even got the privilege of unrolling our banner, and we began to march with pride around the parade deck. The days began to pass quickly, and even the PT was becoming easier since our young bodies were becoming muscled and toned. We had all put on additional pounds of muscle from the rich food that we ate, and we could never get enough. While on PT runs, the DIs sang motivating songs that we joined in signing:

My marine color is gold,
Signifies that we are bold,
Sound off, one, two,
Sound off, three, four,
Sound off, one, two, three, four!

My Marine Corps color is red,
Signifies the blood we shed,
Sound off, one, two

Sound off, three, four
Sound off, one, two, three, four!

Running at five in the morning with a hundred marines, all trying to sing louder than the other platoons running around the same parade deck, competing with them to see who could perform the best, our bodies lean and fit, our spirits high—the experience was exhilarating. I felt so proud to be part of the corps. We sang:

Marine Corps, all good!
Marine Corps, got to make it.
All good, got to make it, Marine Corps,
Got to make it, give me some, PT,
Feels good, PT, give me some,
All day, give it to me, Marine Corps.

Soon we were off to the rifle range, where we would learn how to do our job, shoot our weapon. We recited the "My Rifle Creed." The following verse of the creed captures the essence of being a marine:

I will keep my rifle clean and ready, even as I am clean and ready.
We will become part of each other. We will, before God, declare this creed, that my rifle and myself are the defenders of my country.
We are masters of our enemy. We are the saviors of my life.
So be it, until victory is America's and there is no enemy, but peace!

One of the first things that we learned was not to call the rifle a gun. This was a big sin that you paid for by holding your rifle in front of you at arm's length until your forearms burned and your neck cramped and you could no longer hold it outright. Of course, the DIs would be all over you cussing and calling you names for failing.

Occasionally, a guy would have to hold his dick with one hand and his rifle in the other and say, "This is my rifle and this is my gun. This one is for fighting and this one's for fun."

We learned how to set our sights, "snapping in," as the marines called it, and after we snapped in and tuned our skills, we had only one day to shoot from all four firing positions and qualify on the range. If you didn't qualify, you were dropped from the platoon and had to start over, because every marine was a rifleman and every marine had to qualify on the range. I missed expert by two points and qualified as a sharpshooter. I was just glad to know that I was moving on to the next stage of training.

All we had left in boot camp was a little mess duty, water survival training, and then the big day of drill competition. Of course, I glossed over the water survival training test, which involved being fully dressed and treading water for forty-five minutes in ten feet of water without ever touching the sides of the pool. It wasn't nearly as easy as it sounded.

The end of boot camp was in sight. The constant drilling resulted in increasingly impressive performance. We sounded great marching together in unison on the asphalt parade deck, our boots pounding on the pavement, not a person out of step. And when we came to a halt, our boot heels clicked together with one big pop. We had come such a long way in such a short period, from mooing like cows crossing the same parade deck, not even knowing how to march just weeks ago, to a team of marines. We were proud of ourselves and confident in our abilities. The DIs still picked on us and tortured us occasionally, but you could tell that they were proud of us as well. They even told us as much the night before we graduated, and I realized how I'd grown to almost love these guys. Yes, they had been total assholes most of the time, but we admired them for their leadership in preparing us for war. They taught us how to be marines.

The night before graduation, we received our orders and designation of duty, or MOS, marine jargon for job description. When Gunny started calling them out, I was surprised to hear that only a handful of us were going to be infantry. I thought everyone was a grunt.

"Dark, 0311 grunt. Congratulations, ah-oo-gah! You are going to Vietnam to die." It didn't even bother me when he said it. It was even funny, in a twisted sort of way, because I knew that he was just being himself.

On graduation day were wore our dress green uniforms for the first time. With only six others, I received my first promotion to PFC, private first class. It was only one stripe, but I've never been prouder than that moment. I would wear my one red stripe, which indicated to every marine in boot camp that I was special, that I had excelled, that I could take everything that the marines could dish out. Those big, tough-looking marines on the poster that so intimidated me when Doug and I had joined the corps at the old post office back home didn't have anything on me. As far as I was concerned, I was the meanest and toughest marine on Parris Island, and no one could tell me any differently.

Mom was coming to my boot camp graduation. Dad had started spring training and couldn't make it. It was just as well, because I had never told my DIs that my dad was a professional baseball player, and had they known they might have made me pay!

Graduation went well and we finished second in the drill competition. Once we were done with the ceremony, we were allowed to take our guests on a tour of our barracks. I was alone with my mom when Sgt. David walked in and hollered out, "Hey, Dark, I hear you are a grunt. Welcome to my world, and try not to get killed when you go to Nam!"

My mom just wilted. Sgt. David actually felt bad when she cried. After a visit of a few hours, it was time to tell her good-bye once again, since we would be leaving the next day for infantry training at Camp Geiger.

Doug was going to Cherry Point. Remarkably, the marines took the meanest guy at Parris Island and turned him into a typist. Doug was floored. I was glad for him, since he was going to be a father soon and he might avoid going to Nam. He wasn't so thrilled.

I was done with Parris Island. I'd never return.

Chapter 5

The aim of military training is not just to prepare men for battle,
but to make them long for it.

—Louis Simpson

The bus wandered through the Carolinas on its way to Camp LeJeune.
Once there, I would move on to Camp Geiger to continue my infantry
training. I had heard that we wouldn't be harassed as much and I was
looking forward to a more relaxed atmosphere than we had at boot
camp.

As we drove, I watched the civilians working in their yards, driving
to work, and otherwise living their lives oblivious to what I had been
through. I had changed so much in the past few months that I felt like
a totally different person. For the first time in my life, I hadn't walked
away from a difficult task. Finally I had stood my ground, all alone,
and faced it head-on. I now knew that I could handle life's most difficult and hard times. I was proud of being a marine, proud of serving
my country, and proud of America.

I memorized a quote by Dag Hammarskjöld before coming to boot
camp, thinking that it might help me get through it: "Life only
demands from you the strength that you possess. Only one feat is possible—not to have run away."

In order to be a good marine, you could never run away, and so far I
hadn't. It might sound like a simple thing, but in life it is very difficult
to do.

After we arrived at the base, we were separated into groups bound
for different units. I would spend the next eight weeks learning how to

be a grunt. The nickname comes from the grunting noise that a foot soldier makes when carrying his heavy gear.

At Camp Geiger, I met Harmon Bove. I had seen him at Parris Island a few times. He was the platoon guide for Platoon 102, our sister company. He had the cocky bad-assed walk and the stocky, muscular build to go along with his title of guide. Bove was impressive looking. He was about five feet eight inches or so and two hundred pounds and looked like he could bench-press twice his weight or more. His shoulders were broad and his bulging neck muscles made it difficult to determine where his neck ended and began.

He had been an outstanding athlete from Burlington, Vermont. He had signed a minor-league contract with the Houston Astros as a catcher. He had gone both ways in football, as a linebacker on defense and an all-state fullback on offense. Our new instructor named Bove as the platoon sergeant and assigned him the task of naming four squad leaders. When he saw my one stripe he knew that I had excelled in boot camp, so he selected me as one of the four.

Because of Bove's interest in sports, I told him who my father was. He loved baseball, so the stories of growing up as Alvin Dark's son fascinated him. We would talk about baseball for hours after the day of training was done, and we eventually grew to be inseparable.

One evening I asked Bove why he had joined the marines.

"Well, Dark," he said, reflecting, "I did a very stupid thing. I had a few strings pulled for me and went to sign up with the National Guard. When I went to enlist, to become one of those ninety-day wonders, this dickhead major in the Vermont Guard told me, 'Cowards like you turn my stomach. Young men are dying on the battlefield of Vietnam, fighting for America, while you lie around taking it easy, feeding off this great land.' Well, the son of a bitch pissed me off so bad that I joined the marines the next day." He glanced at me with a big grin. "How's that for being a dumbass?"

I didn't disagree. I told him how I ended up in the corps and how I'd kind of talked Doug into it as well, including how Doug had told me, "No balls, Dark, no balls." We had a good laugh. I knew that I had a good friend.

Our new home was off the beaten path in the deep backwoods of North Carolina. We humped everywhere, usually in full gear, and always with our rifle. When we weren't humping, we were double-timing mile after mile, crawling through barbed-wire barriers with live fire zinging over our heads, or weaving through an obstacle course. We climbed ropes, swung across creeks, jumped over logs, scrambled up nets, grabbed more ropes to heave ourselves over tall wooden walls, stabbed our bayonets into padded dummies, and ran up hill after hill—this was our daily routine for infantry training.

We spent a lot of time firing the weapons that we would use in battle. We threw hand grenades, fired claymore mines, law rockets, and the M79 grenade launcher (blooper, as we called it, because of the sound it made when it fired), the M60 machine gun, and many more. It was cool firing real weapons with live rounds.

We attended endless classes in military strategy—not only attack procedures but how to respond if we were caught in an ambush or captured by the enemy. The idea of being captured had never occurred to me, and the prospect was a bit haunting. One instructor assured us, though, that the enemy would just shoot our dumb enlisted-man's ass. What good would a grunt do them?

Time passed and our hair even grew out a little. I was proud of my new growth, although the marines only let it grow on top. We had to keep it tight on the sides. Our thirty-day leave was fast approaching, and man I was ready to go home. Bove and I had orders to report to Camp Pendleton, California, for final training, and then we would ship out to Vietnam.

It was time to leave, having endured another challenge dished out by the corps that I had passed. Bove and I agreed to meet in Pendleton in thirty days and we both headed home for a much-deserved rest and visit with our families before going off to war.

◆　　◆　　◆

During the plane trip home, I tried not to think about Vietnam. I concentrated instead on spending time with my family, loving them, and being loved in return. I would treasure this precious time together. It would have to last for a year. As my heart pounded, my plane pulled up to the gate in Lake Charles. Then, as I stepped off the plane, I saw my family jumping up and down with excitement. This was the first time that I was able to wear my uniform in public, and even though I only had one ribbon and one stripe, I couldn't have been more proud.

Not everyone felt the same way that I did. The next night I ran into some of my buddies at a local hangout. They sat around with their long hair and careless attitudes, arguing that anyone with any sense would dodge the draft rather than go to Vietnam. Some of the guys I ran into didn't even know that I had joined the corps, but they knew something was strange about my hair cut and couldn't believe what I had done. They thought that I was a weirdo. I began to realize that I had nothing in common with these guys anymore. In fact, it was probably not a good idea to hang out with them, because I didn't need their bullshit to alter my attitude, and as far as I was concerned they were losers. At a dance one night, a guy bumped into me and spilled a drink on me and I wanted to take his head off. My girlfriend pushed me out of the place to avoid a fight. I had little patience with civilians. I actually missed my marine buddies and was surprised at my eagerness to just get on with it and leave for Vietnam. What really pissed me off was how little people even cared about the war. If they could avoid it, so be it. It wasn't really affecting their lifestyle, there was no sacrifice, so who cared.

However, these feelings didn't interfere with me having a good time. I did dumb stuff like just soak in the tub for hours and run more hot water when it got too cool. I slept late every morning knowing that no trash cans would come flying into my bedroom, and I didn't worry about the lights waking me up and someone hollering at me in my quiet bedroom, so I was loving life. I listened to my fan lull me to sleep each night, and when I woke up I threw on my favorite pair of broken-in jeans and a T-shirt. I filled myself with biscuits, pizza, and grilled steaks whenever I felt like it, and I didn't have anyone telling me what to do it or how fast to do it.

I didn't get to see Dad. He and Mom had separated. Baseball season was well underway and he had nothing but baseball on his mind.

I knew that the next twelve months would be hell for my mother. She was certainly going to go through a divorce in addition to having her son in harm's way. I knew that she would watch every newscast about the war and scour every newspaper article about Vietnam. There would be no phone calls once I went to Vietnam, so she wouldn't even hear my voice for a year. Her last thoughts each night would be of her only son, caught up in a horrible war and thinking that he might never come home. Because she watched the news, she knew what I was going to face, and it tore her up inside. I'm sure that to her, the war seemed a senseless waste of human life. Mothers see the world through a mother's heart, and nothing a man can say about war will ever be acceptable to them. Nothing is worth losing a son over. I promised that I would write often, if for no other reason than to let her know that I was still alive.

The thirty days home flew by. At the airport I hugged my three sisters: Allison, the oldest, Eve, who I was two years older than, my little sister, Margaret. They used to call me "prince," because Mom had spoiled me, being the only boy in the family. They were right. I would miss them all.

Saying good-bye was agony for me even though I tried not to show it. In my heart, I believed that I would not return home alive. I don't know why I felt so convicted that I would be killed—or if not killed not make it home in one piece.

I told everyone, "Hey, don't worry about me. I'll do well. Just keep clean sheets on the bed, and I'll be home before you know it." What else could I say? "Mom, I'm afraid that I'm going to die in Vietnam" or "If I come home with my legs blown off, will you still love and take care of me?" Of course I couldn't reveal my dark thoughts. I carried these fears deep inside me, unable to express them to anyone.

I boarded the plane and sat next to the window, watching them wave to me from the gate. As we rolled down the runway, I thought, *I will never see my family again.*

To get through this powerful and emotional moment, I gave myself a pep talk. I realized that if I thought that I would die, then I probably would. If I was going to survive Vietnam, I had to believe that I could. Largely, surviving the war was beyond my control. I could be the best marine in Vietnam and still get whacked. One wrong step, one split second of indecision could end my life. Sitting on that plane, all alone, I prayed to God. I would trust him to guide my footsteps away from the booby traps waiting for me and to deflect the bullets that would certainly be fired at me away from my head. My life was in his hands now. I would survive one day at a time at his pleasure. After I prayed, the burden lifted. I felt at peace, at least for now. I gazed out of the window as the plane lifted over the clouds, and the sun shone brightly through my window. I lowered the shade and closed my eyes and was already missing home.

◆   ◆   ◆

"Staging," as it was called, lasted only twenty days at Camp Pendleton and consisted of getting more shots, getting started on malaria pills, learning about life and culture in Vietnam, and getting back into shape after laying around the house for thirty days. Our activities consisted of humping in full packs up and down hills and sitting through lectures about first aid and treatment of all sorts of wounds that we would witness on the battlefield. For example: What do you do when a marine's guts are hanging out or if a guy gets his leg blown off? As I sat through those lectures it dawned on me that I would probably be in one of those situations, so I paid particular attention. Since I'd never been around bloodshed, I wasn't sure how I was going to respond in such circumstances.

Bove shared my concerns, and being able to talk about such matters with a close friend was comforting. One night we were sitting on the barracks steps having a smoke and started discussing what Vietnam might be like.

"How do you think you are going to react when those gook bastards start shooting at you, Bove?" It was a question I had asked myself almost every day since I joined the corps. "Do you think you will be brave, or will you hide behind anything that you can find, shaking and scared out of your mind?"

"Brave?" Bove asked. "Hell, I'll be scared shitless I'm sure, but I'll do my job." His tone was cocky, sure, and confident. I should have expected such a response from him.

"I'll tell you what I'm afraid of most, Bove." I glanced around and looked up to the stars that were beginning to shine, even though it was still early evening. "I'm afraid of wading out into a wide river, walking point, where the grass is so tall and bushes are so thick on the other side that I can't see the enemy hiding, waiting for me to move into the middle of the river. Once I have reached the center of the river, all hell breaks loose and the enemy is firing his rifle on automatic and rounds are whizzing all around me; I'm in water up to my ass with no cover. There I stand, completely surrounded by enemy fire, and I've got nowhere to go and I stand there waiting to die. I know it's going to happen, Bove. I can feel it." I took another drag then put out my smoke on the steps.

Bove was quiet for a minute. "Yeah, that's a bitch. Everyone thinks about getting hit in a river though, Dark. Hell, it's going to happen to me as well, but hey, it's war, baby!" He wasn't much comfort.

"Dark, do you know what I'm afraid of?" I couldn't imagine what his fear was; he was so strong that I didn't think anything would keep him awake at night. "Do you think you are going to make it through

Nam?" he asked, but didn't expect an answer. "The odds seemed stacked against it, man. Man, we are really going to war! There's no bullshit about it. We are on our way." I just sat there and let him talk.

Bove looked around as if he didn't want anyone else to hear him. For a big, tough guy, he was opening up and letting thoughts out that he had held in for months. "The Nam is no joke. It's the real deal. It's blood and guts and dying man, and I ain't going to make it back. I know I'm going to die over in that lousy piece of shit country. I can just feel it." He took a drag and looked away and started to rock back and forth, a habit he had when he got nervous. Bove's voice sounded cold and cracked when he said that he was going to die. For such a strong, enthusiastic young man, he was surprisingly vulnerable and fragile as he talked about death on the battlefield. All of the rah-rah kick-their-ass rhetoric heard in boot camp to pump us up for war was giving way to self-doubt and fear. We were just two kids thinking about war, and we were scared.

"I see myself dead as well, lying in a rice paddy. I didn't say anything to my family while I was home, but it was like they could sense it." He leaned over closer to me. "I think they could see it in my eyes when I kissed them good-bye, but no one said a word. Death's out there waiting for me, Dark." He glanced at me to see my reaction.

"Bove, I've thought about the same things," I tried to reassure him.

"Wait a minute. I'm not done. I need you to do me a favor ... no, more than that ... I want you to promise me." He pointed his finger at me and tapped my chest. "Will you promise me?" I said that I would promise before he poked a hole in me with his strong finger. "When you get back from Nam, I want you to visit my mother and tell her I was a good marine and that I thought about her every day. Tell her that, at the very least, I served my country, and I tried to do the right thing." He paused briefly. "Then I want you to go to my grave and pour a bottle of Jim Beam on my ass. No bullshit, Dark, I want you to promise me you'll do it." He looked at me with a serious scowl on his face, waiting for a response.

My first reaction was to make a joke, but I knew he was serious, frighteningly so. I told myself that pledges such as these aren't made seriously. They are made on the spur of the moment, not to be carried out, really. I'd go along.

"Come on, man," I said. I told him that he was going to make it and that we would both get through the Nam and that the gooks couldn't touch our mean asses, but my words meant little. I said, "Okay here's the deal, if I die, you go see my mom as well, and if you die, I'll do what you asked."

"You have a deal, my friend." Bove extended his hand to shake on it, and we had a pact.

We went to bed and neither of us brought up the discussion again.

On the first day of July 1969, I calculated that I would be in the bush in Vietnam by the third or fourth. What a way to see fireworks, I thought.

Bove and I went into Oceanside, the town next to Camp Pendleton, and tried to eat everything we would miss over the next year. Then I made the last phone call home and tried to reassure my family that I was going to be fine. I promised to write often. It was a very lonely night when the lights went out. I would miss everything about America. I would miss the pretty, free-spirited American girls, going to a movie whenever I wanted, and watching football on TV on those lazy Sunday afternoons while catching a nap on the couch. For an entire year, I would be in a time warp, far from everything I enjoyed in life.

Soon I was boarding another bus and walking through another airport. As I settled into my seat, I took a deep, halting breath. As I looked out the window as we left American airspace high over the Pacific Ocean, I saw the brown haze of pollution that surround Los Angeles. I crossed my fingers and said another prayer that I would live to see that brown haze again.

As I left for war, I felt prepared, as prepared as I could have been. I remembered something that Bove told me when he joined the marines. He wished that he had asked that National Guard Officer who "insulted" him into joining the corps one question: "Sir, did you serve in combat?" Bove couldn't believe that he hadn't asked that question. Had he asked it and the officer not served in battle, the officer's challenge would have been hollow. Bove might not have joined the marines. I hoped he would make it home. It would be such a tragedy for the world to lose Harmon Bove.

As I sat in my seat, I wondered if the politicians who were sending everyone on this plane to Vietnam had served in combat. Did they know what war was like? I decided that it was a moot point, because the facts were that my ass was on this plane, it was flying into battle, and no matter why I was going, it would be up to me to survive, regardless of why or whom we were fighting. I had to make it for a year, and by God, I'd do it. I closed my eyes and, as I had learned to say when in boot camp, I said to myself, *Piss on it. It doesn't matter!*

Chapter 6

O Lord our God, help us tear their soldiers to bloody shreds with our shells; help us to cover their smiling fields with pale forms of their patriot dead; help us to drown the thunder of the guns with the shrieks of their wounded, writhing in pain; help us to lay waste their humble homes with a hurricane of fire; help us to wring the hearts of their unoffending widows with unavailing grief; help us to turn them out roofless with their little children to wander unfriended the wastes of their desolated land in rags and hunger and thirst, sports of the sun flames of summer and the icy winds of winter, broken in spirit, worn with travail, imploring Thee for refuge of the grave and denied it.

—Mark Twain, "The War Prayer."

We landed in Okinawa, Japan, to reorganize and receive our individual assignments before leaving for Vietnam. I was assigned to an infantry unit, Fox Company, Second Battalion, Fifth Marines, First Marine Division, and Bove was assigned to Echo Company, my sister company. While we would not serve together, we would operate in the same geographical areas during our tour, so I'd at least be able to keep up with him from time to time. The First Marine Division fought bravely at Guadalcanal during WWII, and Fox in particular had been highly decorated thus far in Vietnam.

Bove and I spent our evening at the Enlisted Men's Club to glean whatever information that we could from returning veterans of the war, but most of the guys didn't want to talk about it much, and after witnessing a few fights we decided to go back to the security of our barracks to get a good night's rest before boarding our plane destined for

Da Nang. Once in Vietnam there was no guarantee when we would sleep in a rack with clean sheets, take a hot shower, or get eight hours of uninterrupted sleep again, so we decided to do so while we could.

The next morning, we loaded on another bus and lined up to board our plane for Da Nang. I was starting to get a little nervous that we were flying into Vietnam and had not received our combat gear, and most importantly my M16 rifle. All I had was a seabag with my uniforms and personal gear. Man I wanted my rifle and live rounds, *now!* A few guys who were returning to Vietnam for their second tour assured me there was nothing to worry about and that I'd get my gear when I reported to Fox Company's rear area in An Hoa. They didn't seem concerned, so I played it cool. I wouldn't get nervous until they did.

Within a few hours we were entering Vietnam airspace and everyone became very quiet as all the marines reflected on what lay ahead for them over the next twelve months. I couldn't help but wonder how many on board would not be returning home. I knew thirty guys who were reporting to either Fox, Echo, Golf, or Hotel Company. I hoped that we would all report to Da Nang a year from now and fly home together, but I knew the odds of that happening were miniscule.

I arrived in Vietnam on July 3, 1969. As we taxied down the runway in Da Nang, I was impressed with the fortifications—barbed wire was wrapped around practically everything, and sandbags protected every structure. Marines in combat gear stood watch in bunkers, with their weapons at the ready. The intensity level was definitely higher here than any other military base I'd been to before. The plane stopped, and as we slowly walked down the stairs, a truck loaded with silver caskets pulled up to the plane to load its sad cargo for the trip back to Okinawa. In spite of the heat, the sight sent chills through me.

"They load them up and send them back to Okinawa," a voice behind me said. "The body boys clean 'em up and make sure they look good for Mom back in the world."

He was a big guy, probably thirty or so, and had a big mustache, which was a little odd to see on a marine. He was a staff sergeant returning from R&R. Once you survived the bush for six months you were eligible for a trip out of country for a week, compliments of Uncle Sam. The sergeant swaggered across the tarmac with his hands shoved into his pockets, something that marines were never allowed to do stateside. A marine who walked with his hands in his pockets was called a shitbird.. Evidently in Nam it didn't matter, and he was considered a "salt," a guy who had survived Nam for six months or so. He wore his unpolished boots with pride. A guy's boots told you right away how long he had been in Vietnam. If you had brand new boots, odds were you were new in country, so you were called a "boot." Over here one didn't waste time polishing his boots. I thought it was ironic because in boot camp that's all we did—polish those stupid boots, night after night. This marine wore his cover (hat) cocked back on his head, and his flak jacket was full of holes, with various graffiti on it.

He turned to Bove and me and asked, "Where are you guys going?"

"Fox 2/5 and Echo 2/5, Sarge," I said.

"I'm heading for An Hoa too. Fox and Echo are there. Stick with me and I'll get you guys there. We'll need to catch a chopper." I felt a lot better knowing I'd be with a guy who had been in Nam and knew what to expect.

The Vietnamese were smaller than I had expected, and they smelled terrible—at least to me. Some wore traditional pointed straw hats and loose-fitting clothes, while others were more Americanized, wearing T-shirts and baseball caps. Many women carried heavy loads in buckets hanging from each end of a pole that they perfectly balanced over their shoulders, bouncing down the road in perfect rhythm. A woman approached us carrying her load, and of course Sarge bumped one of her buckets just for fun, which ruined the perfect rhythm she had tried so hard to maintain. He laughed when she started cursing him in broken English, "Buck you, marine. You numba ten!" I figured out the "buck" part and figured the ten meant he wasn't one of her favorites. Her language was sharp and irritating to listen to, and I knew that liking these people was going to be difficult.

We caught a ride to the LZ, or landing zone, on the outskirts of Da Nang. There we waited for our chopper to An Hoa. Bove looked over at me and said, "Where are we going for R&R, Dark?" We were in country for just a few hours and Bove was already thinking about R&R.

"I guess I'll worry about that in six months." Meanwhile I thought, *I hope I have to plan for an R&R. That would mean I made it that long.*

While we waited for the chopper, I pumped Sarge for as much info as possible about going out to the bush.

"Whatever you do, don't sleep on watch. You will get your ass beat for that." He paused for just a second then continued, "And don't fall out on a hump. If you fall out and another marine has to hump your gear, you will be the shitbird of the squad, and every time you get resupplied, you'll hump all the heavy shit." Then he got very serious. "Don't pick up anything off the ground or step on anything that looks funny or suspicious—curiosity will get you blown to smithereens over here. Gooks booby-trap shit that guys just can't seem to resist picking up—don't do it! Just do what you are told without question and you'll be all right."

Just then, a huge explosion rang out, and Bove and I dove for the ground. Sarge laughed at us.

"That's just outgoing artillery fire, guys. The first time you get hammered by Charlie, you'll know the difference between outgoing and incoming."

A marine threw a yellow smoke on the LZ to indicate wind direction for the inbound chopper that was landing. Sarge told us to always get on and off a chopper fast. The chopper plopped down and threw down the back door, and we were motioned to get on with a frantic wave. A chopper sitting on the ground was too easy of a target for Charlie. We hustled on board and sat on a tightly stretched canvas seat. Before Sarge sat down, he removed his flak jacket and sat on it. He leaned over above the roar of the chopper as we lifted off and yelled, "I always sit on it so if we get shot at, the gooks don't hit me in the nuts."

Where was my gear? Here I was flying into An Hoa, which is in the middle of enemy territory and I don't have a helmet, flak jacket, or even a rifle. I didn't get it. Then I realized that Sarge probably said it just to jack with us, and, from the look on Bove's face, he did a good job of it.

The chopper vibrated wildly and the wind swirled through the opened window, where a gunner manned a .50 caliber machine gun. He looked impressive, holding on to the weapon, waiting to blast away into the jungle below if we received fire. Then I noticed something sticking out of his helmet, circled with white paint. Closer inspection revealed a large-caliber round lodged halfway into his helmet. Under the round, the words "You Missed Me" were written. I bet the guy still carries that round with him today, if he made it out of Nam, that is.

As we flew over the countryside of Vietnam, I feared that at any moment I would get my nuts shot off by some gook who took a lucky shot from the jungle below. The terrain below was flat, with rolling hills rising up from the paddies and leading to tall, jungle-covered mountains in the distance. The land had been scarred by endless shelling. Hundreds of potholes served as evidence of the many rounds of artillery fire and bombs that had been dropped. I couldn't imagine what it must be like to live in the middle of this war. I would soon find out.

As we neared An Hoa, the chopper turned very sharply and seemed to literally drop out of the sky. My stomach flipped. As soon as the chopper hit the LZ, the back door dropped open and we were hustled off, a mailbag was thrown at us, and then the chopper lifted off and they were gone.

An Hoa was a fairly large firebase, surrounded by row after row of razor wire. We were warned not to venture near it, since there were hundreds of mines protecting our perimeter. I couldn't image what idiot would venture into the barbed wire, but like Gunny said, "There is always that ten percent."

Bove and I got directions to Fox and Echo respectively and made our way to the compounds. Sarge pointed to the battalion headquarters area and wished us good luck. We wished him the same.

Now it was time for Bove and me to split up. "Bove, my man, I guess this is it," I said, my hand outstretched for a good-bye shake. Even though we were going to be in sister companies, I might never see him the entire time we were in Vietnam.

"I guess so, buddy," Bove said as we shook hands. "Do me a favor you, dumb shit: try to keep your idiot ass in one piece. I don't want to have to go visit your mother. Hey, wait, what do your sisters look like. I might not mind the trip." He laughed.

"Very funny, you shitbird," I shot back. "Try to keep your wide ass together too. I know how hard that's going to be for a stupid catcher."

"Okay buddy, seriously, take care and I'll see you on R&R." Then Bove walked down the muddy road with his hands in his pockets, still walking with that bad-ass walk of his, as if he could have cared less that we were going to war. Then, without turning around, he raised his hand and shot me the finger. Fitting, I thought.

I walked up to Fox 2/5 headquarters along with a few other boots who were joining the company. When it was my turn in line, I said, "PFC Dark reporting, First Sergeant." I stood at attention in front of his desk. His name was Marengo and he was a good-sized marine, probably thirty-two or thirty-three with a crew cut, and although he seemed quiet, I knew he was probably a tough guy. You don't get to be a first sergeant in the marines without being tough.

"Okay, Dark, relax. We don't go for that stiff-assed attention shit over here. Save that for when you get back in the real world." I soon learned how little marines respected the country of Vietnam. It was such a bizarre place to be that they didn't count it as part of the real world, using that term to refer to the United States.

"Where you from, Dark?" That was usually the first thing guys wanted to know about you. Where you were from was the only tie that some guys had to the "real world," so everyone wanted to know where you called home.

"Louisiana, First Sergeant," I answered. I could tell he was disappointed and he continued to shuffle through my paperwork.

"Never been there," he said without looking up. "Okay, you're set for bunker watch tonight. Get some chow and report to the NCOIC for your assignment. Don't go to sleep on watch—we'll kick your ass for that. Report to the armory to get your weapon and gear. You'll be joining the men in the bush tomorrow." Just like that, I was part of Fox 2/5.

I was warned to keep my personal gear to a minimum, because being new in country, the rest of the squad that I joined would probably make me hump some of their gear and certainly the heaviest weapon rounds. I dreaded those frickin' cans of M60 machine gun ammunition; it was the worst to hump. The ammo was stored in heavy metal cans and they were awkward to carry. I had performed the task in infantry training and dreaded the idea of humping the ammo in the bush.

I went to the armory and finally got my M16 rifle, about fifteen magazines, and four bandoliers of M16 rounds. I hurriedly loaded every magazine with live rounds. I would be standing bunker duty tonight and I wanted all the ammo I could carry. Then I picked up a pack, poncho liner, poncho, entrenching tool, a pair of jungle fatigues, two pair of green socks, a dark green shirt and a camo fatigue shirt, two T-shirts, three canteens with belt, a flak jacket, a helmet with a camo cover, about six frags (grenades), a claymore mine, two smoke grenades, a K-bar knife, four C-rations, a few cans of chocolate milk, two bottles of insect repellant (bug juice), a set of writing gear, two flares, a pack of malaria pills, a pack of halazone tablets to purify my drinking water, first-aid bandages, a carton of cigarettes (I had to buy these at a whopping twenty cents a pack), and a rubber mattress to sleep on (called a rubber bitch). I couldn't imagine having to carry anything else. It must have been at least fifty pounds of gear. What more could they pile on me in the bush?

I went to grab chow before I had to stand bunker watch. The food wasn't bad. I wasn't used to eating in my flak jacket and helmet, but it was required in the chow hall.

I reported to bunker watch and shared the position with two other marines. One was returning from a stint in the hospital with malaria and the other was coming back from R&R. Since I was the lowest ranking man, I got the worst times to stand watch. The guy with the most rank took the first and last watch. That way he could at least sleep uninterrupted. I, on the other hand, had to wake up only two hours after going to sleep, stand the watch for an hour, and then the other guy and I alternated hours until one hour before daylight, when the highest ranking guy woke for the last hour of watch. I learned the system.

My first night on bunker watch was uneventful. The flares that were shot high into the air were fascinating. Standing watch, you had to be careful and stay low behind the sandbags, because you never knew when the flare would be shot. When it went off, night turned to day around your bunker and Charlie could shoot your ass. The flares were exploded over the barbed wire periodically, and with a parachute attached, it floated slowly to the ground, illuminating the area enough to see if the VC were trying to get through the barbed wire and throw a satchel charge into the bunkers. Just a few nights before, six VC had approached the wire, but they had been blown to bits after hitting one of the mines—not to mention the marines that sprayed the area with M60 machine gun fire.

I was told that An Hoa sat right opposite of the "Arizona Territory," perhaps the most notorious area of this part of Vietnam, and was separated only by the Song Thu Bon River. It was a very wide river, but during the dry season it became very shallow and the VC and NVA would cross at night and attack An Hoa or drop an occasional mortar round or two into the base just to stir things up. The Arizona was known as a free-fire zone. If you saw someone out of place or things didn't feel right, shoot first and ask later. I guess it had been named the Arizona Territory after the Wild West days in America. Fox 2/5 often operated in "The Arizona," and most of the "hit-the-shit" stories happened there. I was sure that my time there would be memorable, but I wasn't in a hurry to create memories.

I watched a barrage of tracer rounds shoot through the night sky, far off in the distance. As they floated across the sky, they indicated that someone out there was in a firefight. I knew that the next day I could be in the middle of it. While on watch, all alone, I had time to reflect and examine my thoughts.

I remembered an old quote by a guy named James Morrow. "There are no atheists in foxholes." As I sat on watch, I began to pray. I prayed to God to give me courage and that I would not cause the death of another marine. It was strange, but I had a bigger fear of being responsible for the death of another marine than my own death. I was raised in a very strict Baptist family and I had given my life to Jesus at the age of twelve, but regrettably I was never a good Christian, or at least I didn't think I was. Now I felt a little guilty praying for God's mercy, because I probably didn't deserve it. One thing was for sure: I'd probably grow much closer to him in Vietnam, where every day death was so close. I just knew that I couldn't control the future and that constantly being afraid of death was futile. Whatever was going to happen would happen. I would do my best to follow orders, use good judgment, listen to advice, and not get one of my fellow marines blown away. If I did these things, I would have done my best. The thought was liberating in a way and took a lot of pressure off going to the bush. I had a long way to go. Twelve months seemed like a long time to survive in this God-forsaken country.

Bunker watch ended at daylight, when the next shift relieved us. We just had enough time for chow before loading up our gear and heading out to the bush. I loaded up with all my gear and someone handed me the mailbag and I struggled to get on the flatbed truck. I could hardly pull myself up on the truck with all the weight on my back. I felt like a pack mule. I locked and loaded a round into the chamber of my M16, and we were off to join Fox in the bush.

Chapter 7

Anyone who has ever looked into the glazed eyes of a soldier dying on the battlefield will think hard before starting a war.

—Otto Von Bismarck

Charlie often mined the roads in the countryside, so the minesweepers were sent out every morning to sweep and clear the roads before convoys were allowed to line up and move out. I hoped the minesweepers did their job well, but I was relieved to know that at least we weren't the first truck in the line.

A thunderstorm swept through early that morning and left the road a muddy quagmire, so we traveled very slowly, bouncing and sliding through mud up to two feet thick in places. Behind the trucks' cab stood a guy manning a .50 caliber machine gun. He instructed me to watch the right side of the road but not to shoot unless he instructed me to. He could tell that I was a boot and didn't want me shooting a civilian by mistake.

We rambled on for an hour or so. I learned that Fox was performing road security for a few days and then we would be moving toward Phu Lac (6), another firebase. We soon came upon a squad from Fox standing by the road waiting for the convoy. As the truck slowed, I hurled the mailbag to one of the guys and jumped off.

"Are you Dark?" one of the ragged-looking marines asked. He was a small guy with curly blond hair and a very deep tan. He wore his flak jacket over a T-shirt that was full of holes, and his pants were rolled up to his knees. His helmet was cocked to the side of his head and the three-day growth of his youthful beard indicated that life in the bush would not be complicated by strict Marine Corps hygiene requirements.

"Yep, I'm Dark," I said confidently even though I was intimidated.

"The rear said you were coming out. Fall in and keep it spread out. Where are you from, Dark?" Before he even introduced himself, he wanted to know where I called home.

"I'm from Louisiana," I extended my hand to shake his. I didn't take the time to meet everyone else, because I could tell the marine just wanted to move out and get back to the rest of the company. They were set up about five hundred meters off the road.

"Ah-right, another southern boy! Just call me Tennessee." He didn't fit the image of a typical marine. He looked more like a blond Huck Finn. We shook hands and the other marines started to spread out and move in single file.

"Okay, guys, fall in. Let's go, and keep it spread out. Dark, are you locked and loaded?" It was a little embarrassing. I'd been locked and loaded since leaving An Hoa.

"Yeah, Tennessee, I've been loaded up since leaving An Hoa." He didn't respond and I began to move out following the other marines.

The area was flat with rice paddies. The paddy dikes crossed the rice fields, dividing them into rectangles. From the paddies rose small hills that were randomly scattered in between the fields, which were typically covered with heavy brush and trees. I could see farmers huts made of thatched grass partially hidden in the foliage.

Everyone waited until the guy in front of him was about thirty feet away and then fell in silently, needing no instruction to do so. Spreading out was important, because if one guy hit a booby trap, being too close to the guy meant that you too would be wounded. It was also important in an ambush, because you gave the enemy a smaller target.

We humped through a small village with maybe five or six huts and moved on toward the rest of the company. I kept my eyes on the ground, looking for anything suspicious, and occasionally glanced from left to right making sure I was watching the surrounding bush. As far as I knew, we could get hit any minute, but after seeing that the other guys weren't too concerned, I relaxed a bit. I felt secure with these guys but was struck by how ragged they looked.

In training we had been expected to look spit-shined and polished, but these guys had holes in their clothing, and some weren't wearing shirts at all, just their worn flak jackets, and a few had even removed the armored plates so they wouldn't have to hump the extra weight. July in Vietnam was as hot as it got. It had to be over a hundred degrees. However, for a guy from Louisiana, where it was often ninety-five with ninety percent humidity, this weather almost made me feel at home.

Some wore their pants rolled up, and one guy's ass was hanging out of the back of his ripped trousers. I soon learned that no one bothered with the underwear in Vietnam, because it just chapped your ass. Most of the guys needed haircuts and typically they wore it as long as they could get away with. Everyone who could grow stubble on their face let it grow, even though these young guys didn't have much growth potential. And their once-black boots had returned to natural leather from the wear. No boots were polished in the bush.

Their helmets were adorned with graffiti, ranging from peace signs to calendars with each month served in country crossed off. I envied the guys with only a few months left to be crossed off.

These marines were dirty, filthy, and smelled rank, but I could tell they couldn't have cared less. They were used to the stench. Dirt clogged the creases in their skin and deodorant wasn't part of the program in the bush. They were oblivious to the odor. Suddenly I felt very out of place with my shiny boots, fresh new camo clothes, clean-shaven appearance, and white skin, which had not been exposed to the relentless sun yet. My first reaction was that most guys didn't like us "boots." They considered them dangerous to be around because of their inexperience.

In spite of their youth and appearance, these marines were a tough-looking lot. I'd just try my best to fit in and give it time.

We soon made it to the perimeter of our position. As we filed in, the other members of the squad came forward one by one to greet and meet me. Then I went to meet my squad leader, Paul Trenn. He was a corporal. He was maybe twenty years old, but I could tell it was an old twenty. A veteran survivor, he appeared worn and haggard, and like everyone else, his skin was darkly tanned. His hair was bleached by the sun. He was shirtless, sitting in front of his makeshift hooch made with his poncho, boots off, and slumped over a canteen cup of coffee heating up on a little stove made from a C-ration can and heat tabs.

"Sit down, Dark," he said without really making eye contact, which I think he did for a reason. "I want you listen and listen good, because I'm only going to say it once." Now he looked me straight the eyes. "No one in my squad gets another marine blown away because he don't listen to me. If I see you are a shitbird, I ain't waitin' for Charlie to blow you away—I'm gonna shoot your ass myself. Do you get the picture, boot?"

There was no hello, how are you, where are you from—none of that meaningless chit-chat crap—he was a no bullshit kind of a guy.

"Hey, man, I get it," I said as strongly as I could without being a wise guy.

"You'd better believe me that I know what I'm doing. I've been here longer than a whore's dream, and I'll be skyin' out of this shithole soon unless some dumbass boot like you gets me blown away because he didn't listen to me. Understand?" He looked at me again for confirmation.

"I understand, Corporal." This time I just shook my head, feeling as if he didn't know me. I wasn't a shitbird dumbass, as he described me, but I understood that he was trying to make a point.

"You are going to do exactly what you are told by your fire team leader, Donny Clough. You go where he tells you to go, hump what he wants you to hump, and don't talk back or question anything that he tells you to do." He turned back to his coffee. "You'd better pay attention, and then just maybe you'll make it home in one piece." Then he pointed a finger at me for extra emphasis and said, "Rule one: you better not go to sleep on watch. I'll beat your ass silly for that. Second," he held up another finger, "no smoking on watch. I had a guy get shot right in the side of his face one night when he thought he had to have a smoke and Charlie blew off half of his head. All he had to do was aim at the lit smoke. He was a shitbird." He took a sip of his coffee. I wasn't sure if the story was true, but it made sense to me and I wouldn't try to smoke on watch.

"Rule three: always be alert and don't hesitate. A marine who hesitates is a dead marine. I know that you are scared—hell, we all are—but you will do okay if you do what you're told and follow orders. These guys are good and they have their shit in one bag. You carry your weight and you'll get along just fine." I thought maybe he was done, but he went on.

"One more thing, Dark." His voice became more intense. "This war ain't about buying freedom for these gooks—that's bullshit politician chatter, meaningless dribble. This war is about two things: killing those sons of bitches before they kill you and fuckin 'em up before they kill me. You protect me and I'll protect you. This war ain't about medals and glory; it's about blowing away those fuckers who are trying to kill us. We try to kill them and they try to kill us." Then Trenn smiled and said, "Just try and live day after day, one at a time, and pray to God to save your ass and your buddy's ass. You got it?"

I sensed he was done. Once again I affirmed that I got it. If one more guy told me I would get my ass kicked if I went to sleep on watch, I was going to scream. Man, I got it, but I kept quiet. I reached out my hand and shook his strong hand for the first time, and then I was introduced to the rest of my fire team.

A fire team was a group of guys who operated together within the squad. The marines are big believers in structure, and the fire team was the smallest unit in the corps. Donny Clough was my fire-team leader, Bolby was a guy who stuttered badly who I liked immediately, and Tennessee, whom I had already met, was also in my team. As I was expecting, everyone dumped some crap on me to hump just to see what my attitude was going to be. It didn't bother me. I'd do my best. I'd show them I wasn't a shitbird.

Then I met Anderson. "Hey, boot, I'm Anderson." He was from Canada, and as a Canadian citizen, he could have terminated his service anytime that he wanted, but for some reason he stayed and I immediately admired him for it. I met some guys in the M60 machine gun squad who were nuts. They were all from the south and had a confederate flag draped over their hooch, which pissed all the black guys off. Bolby encouraged me to make friends with these people because they could save your ass in a firefight.

I learned that we were in Quang Nam Province. The area was mostly rice paddies, sparsely populated and loaded with booby traps set by the VC.

Trenn came by my position and told me to report to T-Byrd, the platoon sergeant. But first I was to blow up my air mattress. I knew something was up, because I saw a faint smile on Trenn's face when he said it. I pulled out the air mattress and blew it up, getting a little light-headed in the process. When I reported to the platoon headquarters position, a few other boots who had been assigned to other squads were also present with their mattresses.

T-Byrd was a no-nonsense guy who I immediately recognized as someone not to mess with. He was from Texas and spoke with an unmistakable drawl that, being from West Louisiana, made me feel at home. He didn't get to be platoon sergeant by being a nice guy.

"Okay, guys, listen up," he said as he pulled out his KA-BAR knife and waved it around. "No one sleeps on a rubber bitch. They make too much noise and noise gets guys killed out here." He then proceeded to lash out at everyone's mattresses, deflating each one with thrust after thrust. One of the other boots must have found it funny, because T-Byrd grabbed the guy by his throat and pushed him backward.

"Nothin' funny about dying, asshole." He stared at the guy for a few moments to see what his reaction was, ready to beat his ass if need be.

"You guys fuck with me and your ass will forever be in the shitter. I don't even want to hear your names mentioned until you prove that you can cut it out here, and I swear to God, if you go to sleep on watch, you will answer to me. Is that clear?"

He was definitely waiting for a response, and we all agreed that whatever he said went. He brought up the no-sleeping comment again, but I wouldn't be screaming about it—-that was for sure. Not after watching him damn near choke the crap out of the other boot for just smiling. T-Byrd was done with us, and we all knew not to disappoint him.

Trenn sent me to Bolby, who was in charge of me away until I was properly indoctrinated. I'd share everything with him. He was my buddy, and I learned to lean on him to keep me squared away. My first job was to dig our hole, which we used to stand watch in. We heaped the dirt on the front side of the hole for added protection from incoming rounds. Before it got dark, I walked out in front of our position and Bolby showed me how to set out the claymore mines and set a flare with a trip wire that was stretched across a path. I then unrolled the wire and brought back the trigger mechanism and laid it next to the hole that I had just dug. Next to the hole, we placed three frags, ready to hurl just in case we hit the shit.

Before dark, Bolby showed me how to make a C-ration can stove. I used my can opener, which came in the C-ration meal and was referred to as a "John Wayne" by the grunts for some unknown reason, to punch holes in a can, threw in some heat tabs, and my stove was ready for my first meal in the bush. I quickly learned about the pecking order. I got the worst meals since I had the least time in country. The squad leader got first choice. I ended up with beef and rocks, which was supposed to be roast beef stew. It was so bad, and the potatoes so hard, that I skipped dinner and went straight for the candy bar. I also learned how to take a dump in the bush. You took your e-tool (small shovel), went out in front of your position about ten feet, dug a "cat hole," did your business, and then covered it up like a cat. It was a rather degrading and humbling position to be in. You took care of business before dark, because you didn't fumble around taking a dump in the dark. It was a good way to get shot.

Bolby was curious about what I had in my pack and discovered my fresh cigarettes, which I shared with him. I also gave him one of my chocolate milks, which made him a friend right off the bat. He told me my bed would be wherever I lay down, but I had to make it close to the hole so I wouldn't have to go far when awakened for watch. He also cautioned me not to stand up at night but to creep along the ground. A silhouette was a good target in the moonlight.

As it got darker, I settled in for my first night in the bush. Bolby gave me his last bit of advice. "Dark, i-fff-fff," he stuttered, "if the trip fla-fla-fla-re goes off, don't grab the trigger anda-anda-anda fire right away, 'cause sometimes Charlie will sneak up, turn the mine around, and aim it at your position, then pull the tri-tri-trip flare and let-let-let you blow yourself away." That was comforting. So what was the point of the trip flare, I thought?

Bolby answered without me having to ask. "We put-t-t-t-th-those flares out so we can see what's there before we pull the trigger. One night, I didn't put the flare out, and I heard a noise, so I pulled the trigger and bl-bl-blew away a water buffalo. I almost had to pay the farmer for it, and that-that-that woulda pissed me off!" I had a good laugh over that and we settled in for the night.

As dusk settled in, the mood turned more somber. I noticed one squad loading its gear and heading out on an ambush, which we called a stinger. I was very happy not to be going out on a stinger my first night in the field. The squad passed by my position leaving the safety of the perimeter, venturing out into the night, spread out in single file, each guy moving with quiet confidence that came from experience. If they were scared, they didn't show it.

Bolby gave me his final warning about sleeping on watch. He also warned me not to touch anyone to wake them up. A simple whisper was all that it normally took to wake up a marine in the bush. Marines slept lightly. Bolby said that he always slept with his KA-BAR and that his biggest fear was a gook slipping up on him and slitting his throat while he slept, so don't touch him or I might get stabbed. I didn't know if he was jacking me around or not, but I wasn't going to find out.

The hours passed slowly. I stood watch three times, which meant I woke up just about every other hour. When on watch, I sat there staring into the night with my finger on the trigger glancing from side to side, trying to listen for any noise or see any movement. Every fifteen minutes, the guy who was standing radio watch at the lieutenant's position would whisper on the radio, "One Charlie, One Charlie, give me two pushes." We didn't talk while on watch, so to let them know that I was awake and alert, I pushed the radio button twice. It made a squawking noise on the other end of the radio. It was confirmation that all was well.

As I sat on watch that night, I developed a fear that would follow me for the rest of my tour. Way off in the distance, a few tracer rounds shot through the darkness. After a certain distance the phosphorous that covered an M60 machine gun tracer round burned off. The tracer was placed about every sixth round on the ammo string so that the gunner could see where his rounds were going when he fired his weapon. Even though I knew that the rounds being fired that night were far away, I would think, *What if one of those rounds is headed right for my face, right now, and I can't see it coming?* The fear of getting shot right in the forehead worked on my nerves. I stared into the darkness until I couldn't stand it anymore and instinctively, at the littlest noise or perceived movement, I'd duck my head down as if to dodge a bullet. At least I'd make my face a difficult target. If someone had been watching me, they might have thought I was nuts.

The night was peaceful and perfectly clear except for a few clouds that drifted by, which helped pass the time. As my eyes drifted skyward, the stars shone more brightly than I'd ever seen them. The darkness of this desolate countryside enhanced the night sky. I never realized that even though the moon was not shining, the vast number of stars was enough to drape the countryside in a modest blue light. I was amazed that I could actually see the Milky Way. I had never been to a place that was so dark that it could be so easily seen.

As I struggled to stay awake, I thought, *Now I understand how easy it is to go to sleep on watch.* I'd slap myself every once in a while to make sure I stayed awake.

When I looked at the heavens, I thought once again about my creator. I never doubted his existence; even though I wasn't sure exactly what God was, I sensed a presence out here, powerful, mysterious, and magical. Now, because the odds were good that I would soon be standing in front of God without warning, I prayed in earnest that I would be spared and pledged that if I ever made it home, I would appreciate every breath for the rest of my life. My thoughts drifted home, to all of my buddies living their boring lives and taking everything for granted. I vowed that if I did make it home, I'd never take anything for granted again.

Finally, daylight broke and everyone started stirring, making coffee, and heating up a C-ration of choice. Our squad was assigned a patrol through the lowlands surrounding our position. Trenn met with the second lieutenant for his routing and instructed Anderson to get us loaded up. We spread out and one by one, in single file, we started our patrol.

After an hour or so we stopped so Trenn could get a fix on our position. Then after a brief rest we resumed the patrol. Leonard Deane was in front of me, and just as he passed over a small hump in the trail, a huge explosion knocked me backward. Dirt and smoke flew in the air and started raining down on me followed by, "Corpsman up, corpsman up!"

I froze, not sure what to do or even what had really happened, although it was obvious Deane had hit a mine of some sort. Tennessee yelled, "Get your asses out there and form a perimeter," while he rushed by me to tend to the downed marine. Trenn grabbed the radio and was already calling for a medivac chopper. I ran forward.

"Keep those eyes opened, you son of a bitch," Trenn was shouting at Deane, who was going into shock. Although he was black, he was ghostly pale and his movements were getting slower, as if he was fading out.

"You're not gonna die on me, man. Keep those eyes opened. The chopper's on its way man. Hold on. Come on, man, hold on!" Trenn was shouting now. It was a grisly sight, one I could have only imagined before coming to Vietnam. His lower leg was blown off at his knee, and his back and lower body was riddled with holes, some three inches in diameter, as if someone took a cookie cutter and cut flesh off his body like soft cookie dough. The odor of burnt skin and gunpowder filled the air. His pants were literally blown off his lower body and remained attached only at his waist, torn and tattered from the powerful blast. He was turning pale and clammy. The doc showed up and was calm, as if he had done this many times before. I was amazed that despite the trauma done to his body, Deane didn't appear to be in great pain until he started to come out of the shock. Then he began to roll and shake, screaming and growing hysterical.

"Is my leg there, Doc? Let me see, you son of a bitch. Is my leg there?" Doc held him down, refusing to let him up, knowing that would only make matters worse.

"Oh, God, I don't want to die. Doc, is my leg there?" Deane rolled in pain, grabbing his face and shaking. God, I felt sorry for the guy.

"Throw out the yellow smoke. The chopper is almost here," Trenn shouted out. Tennessee tossed out the yellow smoke. Then he turned his attention back to Deane. "Come on, man, hold on. You're going to make it. You have a ticket home, friend. Hang on!" Trenn's voice shook.

Only minutes passed before the chopper arrived. Donny threw out another smoke and the chopper dropped from the sky and swooped in, throwing his back door down. Deane was loaded on board within seconds and lifted off toward Da Nang, trying to cheat death.

We all tried to gather our composure. I knew I was in shock, having never been exposed to this situation before. I knew it was going to happen sooner or later, but I started to shake now. It was odd—I didn't shake during the commotion, but now I was shaking badly, and I hoped no one noticed. I didn't know how to react.

The tension was high, as the marines who were friends of Deane were pissed about their loss.

That night I sat on watch thinking about my day. Thinking about Leonard Deane, a strong young black American fighting for his country and what had happened to him made me angry. I thought that I'd be safe walking that far back in the column, but I now discovered it meant nothing—about five or six guys had stepped over the booby trap before Deane hit it. In fact, had there not been a small hill between me and him, I might have been injured as well. I had my first brush with death, a close call in my mind, but I survived.

To some, the event that day might not have appeared so terrible—I mean, it wasn't as if a bunch of guys were killed in some horrible ambush—but to a nineteen-year-old marine who had no experience with such trauma, I knew I would remember every detail of that day forever. To people who would say, "Oh, that wasn't such a big deal," I say, "Ask Deane how big a deal it was."

I thought about my carefree life at home: how foolish I'd been to get upset when I couldn't use the car on a Friday night date or go out with the guys. I never realized how quickly life could be snuffed out, instantaneously, without warning. I had lived secure from the nightmare that so many others were living—and now I was smack in the middle of it.

I hoped that Deane would recover and have a happy life. I hoped that another mother wouldn't be holding a photo of her son, rocking back and forth, crying about her loss. I also saw the anger in the young faces of the marines on that patrol when the radioman was hit. Had the enemy been present, he would have been dealt with—of that I was sure.

Given the right circumstances—forced to endure tremendous stress, reduced to the lowest rungs of survival, and threatened constantly with death—these marines would quickly and easily become the ultimate fighting machine. That nineteen-year-old high school kid would turn into a coldhearted instrument of death. There is no doubt that the enemy would have been wiped out had he shown his cowardly face.

An enemy that planted booby traps to take the lives of young soldiers didn't deserve my respect. It wouldn't take much for me to grow to hate this enemy. After this day, I was well on my way to hatred. Being shot at, watching that booby trap take Deane, listening to him scream, and smelling the stench of his burning skin and gunpowder was enough to awaken the monster in every one of us. I was learning about war. Vietnam was becoming a reality to me. It would be a long year.

Chapter 8

What a cruel thing is war: to separate and destroy families and friends, and mar the purest joys and happiness God has granted us in the world; to fill our hearts with hatred instead of love for our neighbors, and to devastate the fair face of this beautiful world.

—Robert E. Lee, letter to his wife, 1864

We humped around Phu Lac 6 for a few weeks, then word came down that we were going to the mountains on Operation Durham Peak. It was nearly August. We were going to the Que Son Mountains. Before we choppered out to the mountains, we sat on the LZ waiting for the choppers. Far off on the horizon, I saw my first B-52 strike. I never saw the planes or heard them, but bombs started exploding on the mountain ridges in the distance, and even though we were many miles away from the mountains, the ground shook. The sound was like thunder rolling, and the smoke from the bombs leapt thousands of feet in the air. Hundreds of bombs were exploding one after another, seeming to walk along the ridge of the mountains for miles. It was the most awesome display of force I had ever seen. How could anyone survive such an attack? I couldn't imagine being in those mountains during the bomb drop, and I was glad that someone decided to soften up the NVA before we arrived.

As I sat on the LZ in full gear, sitting on the ground and resting against my heavy pack with the rest of my load sitting next to me, I realized that it was July 20, and Americans were walking on the moon. I thought that as isolated as those astronauts were, I felt just as isolated in Vietnam. I reflected about my experience in Vietnam thus far.

One thing was for sure—I was tired of getting dumped on. The gear weighed so much that just to get up off the ground I had to perform a half roll, then struggle to my knees, then prop myself on my rifle to stand so as not to fall backward. I'd been in country close to a month now, and being a boot was tough. I stood watch at the worst hour; I woke up tired every day from not sleeping well on the hard, damp ground; I got the worst C-rations and was hungry all the time; I got the crummiest cigarettes (usually Pall Malls without filters); I carried the heaviest crap, and other marines always handed me additional ammo rounds to hump along with cans of M60 gun ammo; and I dug more than my share of foxholes.

My gear weighed at least fifty pounds, not counting the crap I had to hump for other guys. The worst part was humping through the mud of the rice paddies. But now I feared that humping up and down the mountain trails would be worse. I didn't weigh 160 pounds, yet I was humping half my weight. I hoped to get a few new boots in our squad soon so I could dump on them awhile. I dreaded going to the Que Son Mountains.

The plan was to give support to the First Marines, who were spearheading the sweep. The veterans told me the NVA had the upper hand in the mountains. Their hospitals, base camps, and command posts were in the mountains, where they could dig into the rocks, safe from the artillery, and where the heavy foliage made it easy to hide when setting ambushes. Supposedly, the bigheaded intelligence guys had targeted a large NVA presence, and we were going to flush them out. I was cautioned that so far we had been dealing with the Vietcong and that in the mountains we would be up against the NVA. They were more disciplined and organized than the VC and typically had more sophisticated weapons. It was a free-fire zone, meaning if it moved, be ready to shoot it. The odds of coming across civilians in the mountains were small.

As we loaded on the choppers and lifted off, I wondered if Bove was on the same operation.

Because choppers had a difficult time landing in the mountains, we came down in a grassy field and everyone immediately ran off and formed a perimeter around the chopper LZ so the next chopper had protection in case we were hit. Once the entire company unloaded without incident, we started forming in single file and began our hump to the nearby peak.

We had been issued mountain rations, which were freeze-dried food in plastic bags reconstituted with hot water before they were eaten. They were much lighter than ordinary C-rations, so we could hump more. Getting resupplied in the mountains was going to be difficult.

When we left the grassy field, we entered the jungle and followed a mountain stream. It was the most beautiful sight I'd ever seen. It was the kind of scenery people would have paid thousands of dollars for at a four-star resort had it not been Vietnam. The jungle was thick, and the heavy foliage reached upward forty or fifty feet, forming a thick canopy that made the surrounding terrain hauntingly darker than it should have been in the middle of the day. The stream was clear as ice, and it rolled easily over large, black, smooth rocks of all sizes, some twenty feet in diameter.

Before we entered the water, Anderson warned us to make sure our trousers were tied to our boots at our ankles, because the leeches would be bad. It was hard to imagine that this clear stream would be full of leeches waiting to latch onto our legs and suck our blood. It probably would have worked had we not had holes in our trousers. Sure enough, when we waded through the stream and took our first break, I rolled up my pants legs and had ten or so leeches attached to my legs. I took out my bug juice that I spread on every night to keep the mosquitoes at bay and squirted a little on each leach. They immediately rolled off, but I was left with a tiny sore. Two weeks later these tiny sores would turn into large, oozing sores perhaps an inch in diameter. We called them "gook sores," and they plagued everyone.

As we moved away from the stream and higher up the mountain, the jungle became less sparse, but it was still thicker than anything I had humped in before. Not being able to see very far on either side of the trail was spooky. If we got opened up on, we'd never see it coming.

As darkness fell, we hadn't reached our position, so the decision was made to simply stop, unload, sit down on the trail, and spend the night in formation. There was no room to do anything else. On the side of the trail, the hill dropped off dramatically, straight down to the stream, which by now was hundreds of feet below us. We wouldn't run any ambushes, and one would alternate watch with the marine next to him.

That night in the mountains was the blackest, longest night I have ever spent. The thick jungle canopy and the low-lying clouds made it seem as if we were inside a closet. I literally couldn't see my hand in front of my face. I just sat there on my watch, staring at the dial of my wristwatch—the green phosphorous on the hands the only way I could tell the time—and when my turn was up, I whispered to Bolby and he stood watch for an hour. I thought that if the NVA hit us that night it would be a disaster.

I don't know why I thought about it, but I remembered what Trenn told me when I joined the squad. He said that the war wasn't about freedom for the Vietnamese but mere survival. If he was right, I began to doubt what we were doing over here. I thought about guys who would certainly be killed and become pale, hollow-faced, dead marines. If the war wasn't about freedom—and it was obvious that the Vietnamese were no threat to the American homeland—could it be true that our reasons for being in Vietnam did not justify losing these fine young marines? Surly it wasn't just a game of survival.

I was a big Bob Dylan fan, and a song that he wrote kept running through my head. Its refrain repeated, "And you know something is happening, but you don't know what it is, do you, Mr. Jones?" Something was definitely happening and it seemed that no one really understood what it was. It seemed that the generals got all fired up about body counts and kicking ass, which then pumped up the colonel, who gave a pep talk to our captain, who then volunteered us for the most dangerous operations. Then we humped our asses off, and here I sat on a trail in the darkest part of Vietnam, squeezing my rifle and whispering to Bolby every other hour so he could sit there squeezing his rifle.

The other thing that was beginning to bother me was that I hated the VC and the NVA, but I was also having a hard time warming up to the friendly forces and civilians. We didn't think of our enemy as a real person. We saw ourselves hunting animals.

If a guy got hit by a mine and some civilians were sitting close by who knew that mine had been there and didn't say anything to warn us, then they got their asses beat. We weren't making any friends behaving like that, but it was a hard position in which to place a pissed-off nineteen-year-old marine who just saw his buddy blown away. What did America expect him to do?

I was glad when the night was over and daylight broke. I felt a lot better and tried to forget the negative thoughts that I had all night long. It was too late to complain. I just needed to get with the program.

After a week of humping, our supplies were depleted. It was hot as hell and our water ran out. The nearest stream was too far away to fill our canteens. It was too dangerous to be wandering around looking for water, so we had to wait for the choppers. At night, we stretched our ponchos out trying to catch the condensation that formed on the bottom side of the poncho from the cool night air. Just enough to dampen our lips made it worth the effort. I never thought that I would ever ask myself, "How many halazone purification tablets would it take to purify my urine, but I did." Finally, before we became half crazed with thirst, the choppers floated overhead with the supplies hanging in a net suspended from beneath the chopper, and then the birds dropped the supplies in our perimeter. Man, we dove into the chow and water.

We finally reached our mountaintop objective and dug in for the night. The view was fantastic, and it was cold. It was hard to believe that in August, which was the hottest month of the year in this hot-ass country, it could be cold. I sat on watch that night, gazing over the valley below, shaking. Vietnam was full of paradoxes.

We were instructed to move out the next morning and our platoon was going to lead the company. Our squad had point for the platoon, and Trenn decided that I would walk point for the squad. For the first time, I was point man. Trenn instructed me to be aware of trip wires across the mountain path we would be following, but since the NVA used these trails often, the odds of booby traps were minimal. The real risk was walking into an ambush, so I had to keep alert for any movement in front of me and if there was any question open up with my rifle.

"Set your rifle on automatic, and if you see movement, blow 'em away, Dark," Trenn said flippantly.

I was trying to imagine the scene. I hoped it didn't happen. We moved out. About three or four hours into the hump, I noticed something odd in the foliage and stopped, then motioned for Trenn to come up to the front of the column. We moved forward and on either side of the trail there were two holes with a trap door made of tree limbs covered with leaves. Surrounding the ground around the holes were footprints. Apparently the NVA had either set an ambush but left hurriedly or were in the middle of preparing for the firefight but caught off guard. Either way, I was lucky. I had dodged one. For the rest of the hump I gleaned the sides of the trail, searching the brush for any signs of an ambush. Thankfully, we finally were off the mountain and I never fired a shot. I had successfully walked point, another milestone for me.

The operation wasn't totally void of excitement. Word came over the radio that one of the other platoons had discovered an enemy base camp and a hospital that would have held a small army of NVA. Apparently, the NVA had excavated under a large black rock and dug a cave deep into the mountainside, safe from the B-52 attacks. Weapons and other supplies were discovered, but the enemy had evacuated before the marines discovered the compound.

◆   ◆   ◆

Once we completed the mountain operation, I began to feel ill. I had lost a lot of weight and felt very weak, as if I had the flu. Then I began to vomit and shake with fever. Doc decided that I probably had malaria.

"I'm going to send you to the hospital in Da Nang, Dark. You get to skate for ten days." Then he called in a chopper and I was sent to the hospital in Da Nang.

I began to hallucinate and I barely remember even getting on the chopper. The only memory I have of the first two days in the hospital is the nurses placing rolls of cotton on my naked body and then pouring alcohol on the cotton and blowing a fan on me to lower my temperature. Between throwing up and freezing my ass off with high-temperature chills, I didn't know if I was lucky to be out of the bush or not. My 105-degree fever finally broke after three days.

I rose up, like Lazarus being raised from the dead, waited until I wasn't dizzy anymore, and then rolled out of the rack and walked to the head. When I stumbled into the head, I saw myself in the mirror for the first time in over a month, and I couldn't believe it. The person that I saw wasn't me. I looked dead. My eyes were sunken and black, and my skin was as pale white as my bed sheet. When I walked by the scale I slowly climbed on. I weighed a mere 135 pounds. I had lost about twenty pounds in a month.

Eventually, my strength returned. One day as I lay in my rack listening to the Doors' "Light My Fire" on the military radio, a nurse wheeled in a guy on a stretcher and placed him in the rack next to mine. I couldn't believe it: it was Bove.

My good friend, Bove, my buddy. How ironic. It was terrific to see him again. He was just what I needed to put me in a better frame of mind. Of course, I had to let him come out of the fog of malaria for a few days, but if he responded to the medication as I had, we would get to spend a little time together before I had to return to the bush.

I decided that for the rest of my stay in the hospital, I'd drink Cokes with ice, eat tons of ice cream, and eat all of the hot chow that I could stand. I was tired of eating those lousy C-rations that were half-ass cooked over heat tabs. I even got to eat in bed. Man, this was like being at a Hilton compared to what my life had been like for the past month. In the hospital, I sat on a toilet for the first time in over a month and stood under the shower until my skin wrinkled, shriveled up, and turned white. After bathing out of my helmet for weeks, feeling totally clean was a luxury that I would enjoy every day.

While Bove was out with fever, I decided to write home. All they had were Red Cross Envelopes, which I knew would give my mother heart failure when she received one, so I wrote on the outside of the envelope, "Don't worry, Mom. I'm okay."

When Bove finally came out of his fever, he rolled over and saw my smiling face. "Well, no shit! If it ain't my old buddy, Dark," he said. "Hey, did you go on that mountain deal?"

"Operation Durham Peak?"

"Yeah, yeah. That was a drag, wasn't it? I got this crap up in the mountains, I guess." He was still groggy from the fever but the next day he perked up. We told each other our war stories, went to a few movies shown on a sheet hanging on a barracks wall, and played cards.

The highlight of my stay was when Ho Chi Minh died on September 2, just three days before my birthday. A few days later, Bove and I celebrated my twentieth birthday with a beer and some vanilla ice cream. I'll never forget my twentieth birthday, in Da Nang, Vietnam, shared with Bove. I said my good-byes to Bove once again, we talked about our R&R plans, and I was off to the chopper pad to return to the bush.

Chapter 9

Once we have a war there is only one thing to do. It must be won. For defeat brings worse things than any that can ever happen in war.

—Ernest Miller Hemmingway

This time I was catching a bird to Hill 65, a firebase where a battery of marine artillery supported our field operations. From there I would catch a chopper out to the bush where Fox was pulling a sweep in a hot-zone—the Arizona Territory. I'd heard nothing but bad things about it, and I wasn't looking forward to going. The chopper swept down, and I loaded up, this time feeling more like a "salt" than a "boot." After all, I had survived malaria, walked point, seen a guy get blown away in front of me, and pulled a mountain operation. Even my boots were turning tan from being in the bush for over two months. I scribbled the twelve months of the year on the side of my helmet and scratched off July and August. Next to June, I wrote, "Split City, baby," indicating when I would rotate back to the "world." The idea of surviving ten more months was still daunting, but my confidence was growing. In just a week or so I could scratch off September.

When the door of the chopper dropped open, I rolled out on Hill 65. I went to the mess hall to stuff myself with my last hot meal for a while. As I was eating, I overheard some guys talking about some Filipino chicks who were going to do a dance for the guys on the hill in a little while. I figured I could probably see the show and still catch the next chopper out to the field; besides, no one would even notice. So I stayed for the show. I wasn't aware of it, but the chopper left for the bush while I watched the start of the show, so I didn't make it out to my unit that night. Instead, I watched some ugly Filipino girls gross out everyone, and before it was half over, I had to leave and report for bunker duty on the perimeter.

As I sat on watch that night, a huge firefight raged in the distance over the Arizona Territory, where I would be going in the morning. I was grateful not to be involved. The marines' tracer rounds, glowing red, crossed through the enemies' green tracers, and the sky was lit by an occasional blast from frags being hurled through the darkness.

The next morning I got the news that our company and indeed my squad had been hit hard and that the company was returning to Hill 65 so I wouldn't be going to the field. Then it struck me that the firefight I had watched the night before might have been my platoon "hitting the shit."

When the company started unloading off the choppers, guys were throwing their gear, wildly cursing, crying, and obviously distraught.

I searched out Anderson. It was obvious from the look on his face that something dreadful had occurred. Anderson was always a calm and collected guy, but he was on the verge of breaking.

He told me the story:

Once Ho Chi Minh died on September 2, the gooks got more aggressive. On September 7, one of the Fox LPs (listening posts that were manned at night) got hit and a couple of marines were killed. The next day Anderson found the VCs' bodies and rifles. Fox was then ordered back to a village that they had vacated a few days before, so they moved out even though it was growing dark and the visibility was bad because of the rain and low cloud cover.

It was pitch black and heavily booby trapped in the Arizona, and any night movement was always dreaded. Our squad led the company into the village and Donny Clough walked point. They also had a dog team leading the way, and close behind was PFC Randall, who I knew only as Tennessee. When the squad closed in on the village the dog froze, indicating there was a good chance that the enemy was just ahead.

Then, suddenly, the night was shattered by AK-47 rifle fire blasting on automatic, firing wildly on the marines. Grenades started flying through the air. Once Fox recovered from the shock of being attacked, the marines returned fire. Confusion filled the night and fierce fighting continued and screams of the wounded pierced the darkness.

When the firing finally stopped and the chaos subsided, Donny Clough was dead, having been hit in the throat by shrapnel, and his legs were both ripped by the blast. Bud Canada, a squad leader who was over half done with his tour, was lying on the ground in agony suffering from multiple wounds on his legs, stomach, and back, and he was struggling not to drift into shock. The dog and the handler were also wounded badly, rolling in pain on the ground next to Canada. Doc was working feverously on the wounded. It was too late to do anything for Donnie. He lay covered with a poncho, and Bolby sat at his side.

T-Byrd took control of the situation while Anderson ran from hooch to hooch throwing frags and firing into the huts with his M16, determined to make sure that the enemy left the area and to release some of his anger and frustration as well. Tennessee was calling in the medivac chopper, and when it finally arrived, he walked up to Doc with a bloody bandage covering one eye and affirmed that he too had taken shrapnel in his eye. He'd been blinded by the impact, so he also loaded on the chopper along with the dead and wounded and raced to Da Nang for medical attention. Tennessee, even though wounded, continued to call in the chopper and perform his duties, not even telling anyone that he was wounded until the chopper arrived. He was tough.

Anderson captured three NVA, two AK-47s and an M16 that they must have taken from a dead marine.

I was in shock after Anderson told me the story. Had I gone to the bush, I might have been where Tennessee was in the column and no doubt would have been wounded or even killed. Bud Canada was severely wounded and now gone. Donnie was dead. It was hard to imagine. He was the guy who welcomed me to Vietnam; he'd been my fire team leader and shared coffee with me almost daily. The dog handler, a cool guy, was wounded badly.

Donny was walking point, which had been my job lately. Would I have been walking point that night? Would I have been killed instead of Donnie? Oh my God, would I be haunted by this episode for the rest of my life, filled with guilt for not being there when my squad needed me most? Should it have been me who got ripped by the shrapnel that hit Bud Canada?

I remembered my fear of being responsible for another marine's death. Was I responsible for one of my fellow marines' death because I failed to return to the bush that night? Had one of them died in my stead?

I later found Bolby and a he had a bleak, stark gaze, which told me he was in shock.

Donnie was his best friend. "Shi-i-i-t, Dark, all he-l-l-l-l broke loose. Donny's dead. My friend is dead." Then he started to cry, and my heart broke. I could tell that his guts were being ripped out of him and he was all alone now, coping with Vietnam without his buddy. There was nothing I could say. I couldn't find any words to express myself. But I could feel my anger inside, growing like a raging, furious beast.

Bolby sat next to Donnie's cold dead body until the chopper arrived and helped carry him onto the medivac bird.

I couldn't face the guys anymore, so I went to be by myself and reflect on what had happened. No one asked me where I'd been that night and why I wasn't on the bird to the bush. No one knew that I should have been "out there," but I knew, and it haunted me. I kept thinking about Donnie's body turning blue from death and Bud lying there in pain and how his life would never be the same again. I thought of Tennessee, blind in one eye, and the dog handler, severely wounded, and I never even took the time to ask his name. I felt hollow, numb, and stunned.

I tried to understand why I had been spared, but it was pointless. War rarely made any sense. The guilt will always be there, deep inside. It seeps to the surface occasionally, and then I cry again. The one night when I wasn't there for my friends would always be a part of my life. Where else but war could a young mind be so twisted by fate, pain, guilt, and heartache?

Have you ever watched an interview of a war veteran? It doesn't matter which war. As he reveals his story, he hesitates and his expression changes, his lips start to quiver, he chokes up a bit, and he is suddenly transported back in time to a horrible event that lives deep inside his tormented soul, and he cries. Maybe now you can begin to understand why he cries.

Is there any doubt why men are so affected by war?

◆   ◆   ◆

For weeks, we followed the same routine of patrol and ambush from Hill 65. The morale was low as we were still recovering from our loss. One day our platoon commander, Second Lt. Williams, shouted for us to load up our gear and report to the LZ. Apparently a recon unit was under fire in the nearby mountains; they were pinned down and needed relief. The recon boys were gung-ho, macho marines who painted their faces in camo and did some wild stuff. I thought it ironic that they needed our help to get them out of a bind.

We loaded up—full packs, gear, ammo, meals for a week—and headed to the LZ. As the day wore on and no choppers arrived, I got really nervous, because nightfall was approaching and I couldn't image how we could fly into the jungle, in darkness, land a bunch of choppers, and unload seventy-five or more grumpy marines—and surprise anyone. This was starting to sound like a very weak plan to me, and I wasn't alone. We sat for another hour and then it got dark. Surely we wouldn't go tonight.

Finally, we were told to stand down—we weren't going. The old Marine Corps adage "Hurry up and wait" was definitely true today, but I wasn't complaining.

A few days passed. Word spread. Captain Furr, our company commander, had solid intelligence that a recent *chu hoi* (a defector who now worked for the good guys) knew where the VC had hidden a stash of mortar tubes. It lay just on the other side of the Song Vu Gai River, not far from Hill 65, where we were stationed. So Captain Furr decided that we would take the *chu hoi* and have him lead us to the weapon stash.

The VC used mortars very effectively since they were easy to carry, could be set up quickly, and used rounds that were not excessively heavy, so even the VC women could hump them. They inflicted serious damage to troops when accurately fired, so Captain Furr thought it was a good idea to pursue them. I had my doubts about how reliable these *chu hoi* characters were. They could be decoys leading us straight into an ambush.

My squad was elected to walk point for the patrol. As we got closer to the river, a conversation that I had with Bove back at Camp Pendleton before coming to Vietnam flashed in my mind. My biggest fear was wading out into a river and walking right into an ambush with no cover. I started feeling bad about the captain's plan.

As we approached the river, it was agreed that Bolby would walk point. I was second in line. Bolby would make the VC defector walk just in front of him, and for good measure he grabbed the VC by the back of the shirt and I could hear Bolby stuttering to him saying. "I-i-i-if I so much as even h-h-h-hear a shot or anything th-th-th-th-that sounds like a shot, your ass is dead." I doubted that the VC even understood English much less Bolby's version of it, but one thing was certain: he understood Bolby's inflection and the rifle pointed at his head. I knew Bolby was scared, with the memory of Donnie still fresh in his mind, but it was still comical hearing Bolby try to spit out the threat to the VC.

The river was wide but shallow. It was late summer and the dry season. The current was slow and there were small sand bars poking out of the water, with sparse vegetation and grasses growing on the exposed soil. The Gai was probably two hundred meters wide, so as we moved into the river we would have no cover. In the distance, along the other bank, elephant grass grew four to six feet tall, so thick that it looked like a wall. If the VC were in the grass waiting to ambush us, they would not be detected until the fire from their weapons gave them away—and that would have been too late for us.

My stomach was not feeling good about this at all. I had an eerie feeling, wading into the river, walking behind Bolby, who was still muttering to the VC, who was already up to his knees in the cool river water. I readied my rifle, off safety, finger on the trigger, all of my magazines loaded and ready to be swapped out. If we hit the shit, I would be ready for the worst.

The rest of the squad was moving into the river behind us, and when I got about halfway, the barrage of enemy fire filled the air. At least a dozen rifles were howling on full automatic, their loud KAK-KAK-KAK noise unmistakably marking them as AK-47s. It seemed that thousands of rounds were flying by my head so close that I could feel their heat as they whizzed by, skipped into and off of the water, thudded into the sand bar around my feet, and threw up sand in front of me. It was crazy and bizarre.

We started firing back, unloading our weapons in seconds, dropping the empty magazine and slamming another in and spending those rounds as well. I dove behind a clump of grass on a sand bar, as if that was protection. Then I saw Bolby trying to grab the VC and at the same time running backward toward me.

He gave up on the VC and hollered, "Back, Dark! Haaaaa-uuul ass!"

I got the picture. As he raced by, the VC defector wasn't far behind. I felt like shooting that bastard. I continued to fire my weapon, then jumped to my feet and raced back into the knee-high water and struggled to wade back to our side of the river.

Rounds continued to fly all around me, and when I made it back to the friendly side of the river I dove behind cover and lay there trying to catch my breath. How had I not been hit? It was incredible. We began shouting and screaming and continued to fire our weapons toward the VC on the far side of the river.

Then, all was quiet.

My heart was pounding and I could hardly breathe. Finally, I began to take in deep breaths and began to shake, much as I had when Deane was blown away. Adrenaline kicks in when fighting, but once the terror is over, the realization that you almost died kicks in and then your mind becomes afraid.

At the time the rounds were flying by my head, it was exhilarating in a weird way, perhaps the biggest rush I've ever experienced. There was an odd sense of freedom from everything normal as I wildly fired my rifle, unleashing all the power of my weapon on a hidden enemy, releasing pent-up hostility, wanting to kill the enemy to get even for Donnie, Tennessee, and Canada, shouting and screaming obscenities, not even caring if I got hit, not even feeling vulnerable, as if I were invisible—while everyone around me went insane. It was the most stimulating feeling that I ever had, but now I was shaking with fear realizing that I probably should have died in that river. But I survived.

I had just lived through my greatest nightmare, and it was empowering and I felt good.

The firefight is a very seductive and powerful feeling in war. Was it possible that such horrifying circumstances could be so stimulating and even satisfying? Ask any combat soldier, and if he has been in a firefight, and if so he will tell you how exciting and exhilarating the experience was. Nothing in civilian life comes close. I will never forget the sound of those rounds flying by my head, that eerie zinging sound that still echoes in my ear.

Chapter 10

The battle, sir, is not to the strong alone; it is to the vigilant, the active, the brave.

—Patrick Henry

We moved off Hill 65 back into the bush and set up east on Hill 37. We were getting off the beaten path and operating in a more dangerous area. We were very close to the Arizona Territory, so the VC and NVA were close by. The farther we got from a firebase, the braver Charlie felt.

One morning after returning from the morning strategy session with the lieutenant, Anderson told our squad to pack our gear. We were heading for Charlie Ridge to run a patrol and then set up an all day observation post. I didn't like the name "Charlie Ridge" which obviously got its name because the enemy had an affinity for the location. It was going to be a long hump up the side of a mountain. We'd find a small hill to set up on and would spend the day scoping out the mountainside for the enemy. I was a little concerned that if we hit the shit, we would be at least a mile away from the rest of the platoon.

Anderson asked me to walk point and off we went. There were no villages in this region and the ground was not farmed, which usually meant that the area was more volatile. I would be extra vigilant. We moved on with the patrol and it was uneventful as we made our way to a small hill separated from the larger mountainside by a narrow ridge. Anderson decided this was the spot he had coordinated earlier with the lieutenant. He directed us to spread out and take cover, hiding in the scrub-brush so our enemy couldn't detect our presence.

On this patrol, we took an M60 machine gun squad with us for added firepower. Anderson had also coordinated our position with the mortar guys before we left on the patrol so they could be ready if we needed them. Anderson radioed the platoon that we were in position and we simply waited for the enemy. The day was sunny and we settled in not really expecting anything unusual to happen.

Hours went by. Then Lee, a recent boot who had joined the squad some weeks ago, suddenly pointed to his right, mouthing out, "Gooks."

"Get down and be still," Anderson said as he scooted along the ground in a crouching run toward Lee's position. I was next to Lee, and I saw what he was motioning about. Across from the hill we were on, the ground sloped down to form a small valley and then back up the mountainside. In a small opening, a cascading waterfall broke out of the brush. It was in plain view. In the waterfall stood two NVA taking a shower, and we could even hear them laughing. They were maybe 150 meters away.

Anderson wanted to open up with maximum firepower, so he instructed everyone to lock and load. The M60 squad couldn't wait to unload on the unsuspecting enemy. We all took aim and waited for Anderson to motion to let the rounds fly. Anderson called the lieutenant to advise him of our situation and that we were about to open up on the NVA. Then he raised his hand and dropped it, making the gesture to fire.

Everyone started firing, and it looked like one of the NVA in the waterfall fell, but in the excitement and because of the distance, I wasn't sure. We sprayed the entire mountainside with our weapons, and then we received enemy fire. Rounds were hitting all around us, and from the volume being heaved at us, I thought they might have a machine gun as well.

Anderson was on the radio and it was clear that he was calling in mortars. Soon we heard the whistling sound of a mortar round flying over our heads and slamming into the mountainside. The first round is always a white phosphorous round to spot the location. If it hit the target, Anderson would tell them to fire for effect. If it fell short and was too close to us, he could add more meters and fire another spotter round. The first one was accurate enough, so Anderson screamed over the radio, "Fire for effect!"

We continued to fire our weapons, a little too much for Anderson, who yelled, "Cease fire, cease fire! Give the mortars time to work and save your ammo."

When the mortars stopped, we rose slightly to see if we could see any movement, and more enemy fired erupted from the mountain, striking one of our guys in the boot heel. We opened up again. Then it got quiet.

Anderson wanted us to make a run up the mountainside on the small ridge that led to the enemy position. We scurried, and the enemy unleashed fire once again, so we retreated down the path on the ridge to our position as rounds were bouncing off the rocks and leveling some small trees surrounding us. We dove for cover behind the many rocks that surrounded our position.

Then, for additional support, Anderson called in a gunship to mow down the side of the hill before we made another run. When the gunship arrived, we were in for a spectacular sight. His rounds blasted the side of the mountain, devastating everything in its path. After the gunship worked out on the side of the mountain for a few minutes, it grew quiet once again. No one could have survived that volley of rounds, I thought.

We mounted up and headed up the path. This time no fire was returned. We found nothing. No bodies. That wasn't uncommon, since Charlie always tried to remove the bodies from the battlefield. We did find spent round casings. The enemy had disappeared somehow. Probably through a network of caves, although the jungle was thick enough to provide cover for a quick retreat. I was just glad that it was over and no one was wounded.

Anderson didn't want to chance another attack while we were in such an exposed position; and besides, the mission was accomplished, so we mounted up and started the patrol back to the platoon before it got dark.

I didn't walk point on the way back, so I had a little time to think about the events of the day. I noticed that I didn't shake after the fire-fight this time. Could I have been getting "used to it"?

My respect for these marines soared. Anderson was a hell of a leader, and he had his act together. We could trust him, and I admired him tremendously. All these marines were real men, even though we looked like a bunch of kids. What kind of men would charge up a narrow path without cover, determined to kill the enemy, knowing they would be fired on, for no other reason than their squad leader ordered them to? These guys were heroes to me. Everyone was scared, but they did their job. They laid down their lives, and I was so proud to be part of their squad. These guys were the meanest, toughest sons of bitches I'd ever been around, and I was one of them!

I remembered what Gunny told us in boot camp—that we would be the meanest pricks ever to leave Parris Island. It took a while, but now I felt just that tough. No one in this squad was a boot any longer.

Exhausted, we continued to hump down the mountain back into the safety of our perimeter. It had been a long day. As a reward for a job well done, we didn't have to stand watch that night. I couldn't believe that I would get a full night's sleep, uninterrupted.

◆   ◆   ◆

The next movement that Fox was assigned would be highlighted by one of the most terrifying nights of my life. We were going back into the Arizona. We were going back to the village where Donny had been killed. Our squad would lead the platoon; it would be a night movement to surprise the enemy, and I would walk point. In addition, since we were moving at night, we had to stay on the paths or we could easily get lost, and if we tried to go through the brush, we would make too much noise and there would be no surprise.

At night, I wouldn't be able to detect a booby trap buried in the trail or see a trip wire stretched across the trail as a trigger. The VC took a C-ration can, attached it to a stick, planted the stick in the ground on the side of the trail, wrapped a wire around the head of a frag, pulled the pin on the frag and slid it into the can. Once it was in the can, they pulled the wire across the path and attached it to another tree on the other side of the trail. The device was very effective, since at night a marine couldn't see the wire, and if it hit his pants he couldn't tell it from just another branch sticking out into the trail. When he hit it, the grenade fell from the can and detonated, normally blowing away the point man and the marine next to him.

We didn't have a dog team to detect whether the enemy was in the village. To complicate matters, it began to rain and the clouds hung very low in the evening sky, so once it got dark, it would be almost impossible to see. I couldn't imagine a worse scenario. I began to believe that I was going to die tonight. There was no way I was going to survive. I had dodged death the last time, and now fate was going to get even.

The Arizona was relatively flat and surrounded by the Son Vu Gia and the Song Thu Bon Rivers. The Vietnamese who lived there were isolated, backward, almost living in the stone age, constantly torn between harboring the VC and NVA and trying to eke out a living from the war-torn land. They were trapped in the middle.

We moved out. Anderson appreciated what we faced, what could be waiting for us. My spirits sank, but I moved on, leading the squad. Hours went by as we silently glided through the countryside. It grew darker as we got closer to the village.

The darkness seemed to fall quickly, hastened by the clouds and the light rain that soaked my helmet cover and dripped off the brim, occasionally sliding into my eyes. I glanced from side to side trying to detect any movement in the brush on either side of the trail and strained to see a trip wire waiting for me, but it was too late for that now—the darkness would conceal death.

As I moved down the trail I began to shake. Then, without thinking, I was recalling the Psalms that I learned as a kid: "Though I walk through the valley of the shadow of death, I will fear no evil. Thou dost prepare a table before me in the presence of my enemies. Thy rod and thy staff comfort me and I will dwell in the house of the Lord forever."

My spirit was bolstered, but only briefly. I quickly sank back into depression. I wasn't sure if I could continue. My courage was fading.

I continued to march as we closed in on the village, waiting for the "click" that I would hear before the mine was triggered under my foot. I glanced from side to side, my rifle set on automatic ready to fire into the darkness. All I could imagine was Donnie turning blue and Bud Canada lying in the mud wounded and moaning. I was sure I would find the same fate.

With each step, I expected to hear the explosion of the booby trap that would take my life or blow off my young legs. We were getting close now—maybe fifty meters or less. I saw the dim light of fireflies and I almost opened up thinking it was a gook smoking. Then I froze—my legs wouldn't move. I heard a whisper from behind me.

Lee tapped me on the shoulder from behind. "Dark, lieutenant says move out."

I turned to tell Lee to pass it back to the lieutenant that if he wanted to move quicker, to get his chicken-shit ass up here and he could run into the village as fast as he wanted. I couldn't speak; I tried to but nothing came out. I started shaking so violently that I couldn't move. My mouth just quivered. Tears stung my eyes as I glanced back at the tree line surrounding the village, and I prayed silently to God, "Lord if it's my time, take me quickly. This isn't human. No man should have to go through this. Remember me, Lord."

It's hard to describe the feeling, but it was as if I'd died. I wasn't even on that trail anymore; it was as if I had been lifted above the scene, although I knew I was still there. I found the courage to move forward, one step at a time. If I set off a booby trap, or if the gooks opened up on me, it was out of my hands. These dirty bastards weren't going to make me feel like this. I was above it. Feeling death this close was liberating.

Here I am. Take me if you can. But I'm walking into the village, and if you're waiting for me, I'll take as many of you with me as I can.

I stopped shaking, my legs found the strength to take another step, and I steadied myself and moved into the village. Nothing happened. The enemy wasn't there. No one had been hurt. My legs were still attached to my body. I had been spared. I slumped to the ground completely spent, exhausted from fear.

To everyone in the column, it had been an uneventful movement. The only comment was, "Why were we moving so slow—and now we have to sleep in this freaking rain!"

I slumped on the only high piece of ground I could find, placed my head in my helmet, lay on my side, covered myself with my poncho, slid it over my head, and slept. It had been the most exhausting night thus far in Vietnam. But I knew the experience had given me strength.

I had transformed that night, and I was forever changed. When I reached out for God, I found him. He gave me the strength to get through that night. He was there. I could feel it. Many people go through life never finding God or realizing that, yes, he is there. He showed himself to me that night, in the darkness, in the Arizona. In that instant when I stood all alone, shaking on that trail, about to break, he comforted me. He was all around me, as if angels were holding me up, bolstering me with courage, protecting me, and he gave me the power to move forward into the darkest night of my life.

I also discovered what I had inside, deep down in my soul. When I was convinced I was about to die, I didn't run away. I remembered a quote I had memorized: "Life demands from you only the strength you possess. Only one feat is possible—not to have run away." I froze, but I didn't run. I moved into that tree line and no one knew how scared I was. Finding the courage to walk into that village was a personal victory.

I also learned something good can come from the worst situation. When we faced tough times in Vietnam, we said, "What more can they do to us? Shave our heads and send us to Vietnam?" Well, nothing could have been more terrifying to me than the night that I just had. I would now be prepared for just about anything else that could happen to me for the rest of my tour in this hellhole.

I also swore to myself that if I made it home, I'd never let life get me down again. All I need to do was remember this night in Vietnam to pull me out of any pit of despair. For the rest of my life, I would remember what it was like to walk into certain death and live.

Chapter 11

Victory belongs to the most persevering.

—Napoleon Bonaparte

The monsoon was upon us. I had already scratched off September and October on my helmet and would soon be able to place an "X" by November. The monsoon was Vietnam's version of winter. It came shrouded in damp, dreary clouds that hung low on the horizon, covering us like a blanket. It often rained every day for weeks at a time. The marines began to get a haggard tired look on their sullen faces. We were depressed from sleeping in the rain. We were constantly bored and wet. All we had was a poncho to keep us dry.

Our T-shirts literally rotted off our backs from the sweat, mud, and lack of bathing or washing our clothes for weeks at a time. Our feet swelled with immersion foot. The skin turned white, rotted, and fell off your feet from being wet all the time, leaving big, raw sores. Walking became impossible. We tried to take our socks off to let our feet dry, but it wasn't a good idea to have your boots off if we got hit. I was sent to the hospital for ten days with it. When we received clean, dry socks, it was like heaven to slide them on our disease-plagued feet. Malaria was also rampant.

Cuts turned into oozing gook sores. Even the guys with dozens on their legs were not sent to the hospital, because they didn't keep a soldier from fighting. If you could hump, you could fight. The doc would flood the sores with iodine to soothe them, but the constant dampness prevented them from healing. I still have two scars thirty-seven years after leaving the bush. As the endless rain pelted our helmets, we slumped over canteen cups of hot chocolate simmering on the heat-tab stoves and tried to stay dry. Sleeping in the monsoon was most diffi-cult. We often teamed together, joining our ponchos to one another to form bigger hooches. We dug a little trench around the perimeter of the hooch so the rain would slide off the poncho, down into the trench, and away from your hooch, keeping the ground beneath you dry. Of course, the plan didn't work when the rain came down heavily. It simply overwhelmed our engineering.

Going on a nighttime ambush was worse. You had to stay alert, which meant draping your poncho around your shoulders and cover-ing your gear, taking a position in the brush, and simply leaning against something to sleep. I often sat in water all night and learned to sleep on my side so that only half my body got soaked. While on an ambush, we spread out about five feet apart next to a trail that the enemy might have been using and simply waited for Charlie to walk by. We never stood up at night. A marine's silhouette against the night sky provided a target for Charlie.

Pulling our turn on watch was tough as well. Your eyes played tricks on you. Grunts had to be alert for any sign of activity. The falling rain moved the vegetation, so detecting the enemy was almost impossible. Our vision was limited to about ten feet, and the sound of the rain hit-ting our poncho masked the noise of the advancing VC. I hated the monsoon.

◆   ◆   ◆

We were set up once again next to the Song Vu Gia River, but now the current was strong and the river was swollen by the monsoon rains. As I was changing socks, I saw a hand suddenly jut out of the water, being carried swiftly by the current. A group of frantic villagers raced along the bank next to the river following the hand, screaming, crying, and pointing.

Without thought, I found myself diving into the river swimming out to reach for the tiny hand. The current was stronger than I had anticipated, but I managed to get to the hand just before it sank out of sight. I grabbed the hand and yanked it up. A tiny girl was fighting for her life, but I couldn't tell if she was already gone. I pulled her against the current as I made it to shore. Once on the bank, I mashed on her back, trying to push the water from her lungs. Suddenly she coughed, gasped for air, vomited, and started to cry.

She was a little girl of maybe seven or eight. Her color started to return, filling in the pasty blue she had been just a few seconds before. She would be all right. Just then her mother raced up to me and violently but lovingly hugged me. She was so small that she barely reached my waist and she was crying in appreciation. Then she dropped to the ground and started hugging her daughter, who by now was reaching for her as well. Her father held his hands together, bowing before me, jabbering in Vietnamese, which I couldn't understand a word of, but I could tell that their hearts were full of joy; their daughter was safe.

For the first time since coming to Vietnam, I realized that these people shared the same emotions that I did. They loved their family as I loved mine. Until now, I had been consumed by hatred; I had stopped thinking of these people as humans. How many times had I brushed them aside, cursing at them to get out of my way?

I recalled during a patrol after Donnie had been killed when we passed by a hooch filled with Vietnamese. An old woman was cooking her meager meal for her family in a big pot over an open fire. I was so full of hate that I walked over to the pot and pissed in it. How could I have done such a thing? War does that to you. You become a different person. In no other circumstance could I imagine doing such a thing.

Now I was surprised that I felt so good about saving that little girl's life. I often think about her. I wonder if she made it through the war and, if she did, what did she do with her life? Does she have kids of her own, and does she still tell the story of how an American marine saved her life on that dreary day when she almost drowned? I knew that her parents would never forget.

Maybe years later, when the communists took over, no matter what the parents were told about the "American Devil," they would still secretly love America because of that fateful day when one marine saved their little girl from the swollen river.

I was trying to take lives and my most rewarding experience thus far in Vietnam was not the result of violence but of saving a life.

◆   ◆   ◆

I was meritoriously combat promoted to lance corporal. Anderson said I had proved myself in battle, and coming from him that meant a great deal. I also got another fifty bucks a month.

Robert E. Lee had been in the squad for a while, and I grew very close to him. He was from Tennessee. He was stocky and didn't have a lot to say, but he was tough. PFC Cobb also joined us, and he was also a southern boy. I nicknamed him "Water Buffalo." Cobb wasn't afraid of much, and he was so big that his pack looked like a wallet on his back. He could hump anything. He always found something to laugh about and was a great asset to the squad. John Gary became a member of the squad; I called him "Opossum" because of his short-cropped, sandy, prematurely graying hair. He was sharp and never got lost. Starkey was from Arkansas. He was a solid, dependable guy. He never complained, just did his job. We all bonded immediately.

Stateside, I'd heard that the war was being fought by the poor, but that just wasn't so. We had a cross-section of America represented. We had attorneys, medical students who had flunked out of school, construction workers, a few surfer bums, and a motorcycle gang member—just about any walk of life you could think of. We were just average kids, thrown together by circumstance.

I checked off November and soon December would be scratched off as well.

It was still the monsoon, miserable and wet. Word was passed that Fox was on the move again and we would be part of a massive sweep along the Song Vu Gia River. Once again, our fate would be tied to the now infamous river. Our squad would be closest to the riverbank. Once we arrived at our destination, we lined up parallel to one another and started moving through the elephant grass. If you got more than ten feet from the marine to your left or right, you lost sight of him.

Suddenly I heard rifle fire and hollering coming from the riverbank. We turned and raced in that direction, struggling to find our way through the tall grass. When I arrived, marines were lined up along the bank shouting and firing their weapons. NVA were being dragged out of the elephant grass, and the ones who were trying to get away were being shot as they tried to swim under water for their freedom. One by one, the NVA hiding in the grass stood up holding their hands in the air muttering halting Vietnamese. I stood on the bank firing into the water at shadows, like giant fish trying to swim away from the firefight.

Officially, we were told later that we had killed twenty NVA and captured twenty-eight. I think it was more than that, because there was no way to tell how many floated down the river. When the firing stopped, we huddled the captured NVA in a tight circle, tied their hands, and made them sit quietly. We then searched them all. There were many women in the group and the search revealed that one of the girls had hidden a medal in her vagina that she had been awarded for killing marines. That didn't go over very well. As I often wondered when the captured NVA were flown to the rear for their interrogation, did she make it, or did she disappear mysteriously as the chopper flew over the desolate Arizona Territory?

Christmas was fast approaching. I scratched off December even though I had another week to go. Fox was heading to the rear for the first time since I got to Vietnam. Anderson was also rotating home, done with his tour in Vietnam.

"Dark, I'm making you squad leader. Take care of these guys. I trust you with their lives." I was surprised at the promotion, but I told him to not worry and that he owed it to himself to get out of this place as fast as possible. On the way to the LZ, he turned to me and said,

"Dark, I didn't make you walk point because I didn't care about you—I trusted you. Can I trust you with their lives?" He said this very seriously and wanted a serious response.

"Yeah, man. I'll do my best. Take care, my friend."

"You guys are my family. Just take care of my family." He slapped me on the back and said that he would write. He then loaded on to the chopper, and was gone.

Most of the time when a guy said he would write it never happened. When a marine left the bush it was too painful to think about the men he left behind. No one wanted to know who got wounded or killed after he left. It was better to forget the bush, stash it deep in the back of your mind and go on with life. I'd probably never hear from Anderson again.

Now I was the squad leader. I was half done with my tour, with six months to go. It seemed like a lifetime. My new responsibility weighed on me. However, it had its perks. I got the best C-rations, best cigarettes, and best hours on watch. I didn't dig foxholes anymore, and no one gave me any crap to hump.

We had a new second lieutenant, Maley. He was a good guy. He had a heavy black moustache, which was unusual for a lieutenant. He met with all the squad leaders and told us that he would rely on our experience to help him adjust to the bush. This was his first tour of Vietnam. A lieutenant only stayed in the bush for a six-month tour. I never quite figured out the policy; we needed experienced officers, and just when they figured out Vietnam, they rotated and we got a new one. Maley was my third platoon commander.

On my first patrol as squad leader, we made a move to Go Noi Island. It was another badass area, sparsely populated, heavily booby-trapped, and home to the VC and NVA. It was very low and susceptible to flooding from the large Song Ky Lam River, which partially encircled it. There were very few villages in the area, and once again it was a free-fire zone for us. But we were cautioned that there were still a few civilians living in the area. The officers told us, "We don't need any complications here—make sure you have a good reason to zap them."

We left from Liberty Bridge and moved east toward La Bac, a small village. The moving was slow because I refused to use the trail. Surely, it was heavily booby-trapped and I wasn't taking any chances. It was my first time leading my squad. We waded the paddies instead. After about an hour, word got passed up to get our ass back on the trail and that the colonel wasn't wading the frickin' paddies. I ignored him, and when we reached the objective without casualty, I got an earful, but everyone was safe. What would they do to me? Shave my head and send me to Vietnam. I'm shaking!

After reaching our objective just outside of Lac Bac, we set up camp. The next morning on January 16, 1970, we woke from a good night's rest and everyone made chow, drinking coffee and getting ready for the day. Without warning, an overhead round burst over our position, then another. My first thought that we were getting hit by friendly fire, but when AK-47s opened up on our position I realized that Charlie was attacking. I grabbed my rifle and started crawling for cover and returned the fire in the direction where I thought the gooks were. Another burst went off overhead and I felt a stinging in my right hand. A piece of shrapnel struck the meaty part of my hand between my thumb and forefinger. It was hot as hell but only a glancing, superficial wound. I jumped up and started firing on automatic, getting more and more pissed. Those bastards hit me and I was ready to get revenge. But as usual they were nowhere in sight and all became quiet as suddenly as it started.

We were ordered into formation to begin a sweep of the area. A medivac was called in for the wounded. As I went to see doc for some iodine for my hand, a guy was lying on a stretcher with a large-caliber round lodged halfway into his skull, protruding out the back of his head. He was lucid and, smoking a cigarette, although he was fully aware that he had a round stuck in his skull. I couldn't resist asking him the obvious.

"Hey, doesn't that hurt, man?"

He glanced at me, not moving his head.

"No shit, man," he said, as if I was the biggest dumbass in Vietnam. What a war story this guy would have the rest of his life. I bet he still has that round mounted on a trophy somewhere.

We lined up and started the hump. Our squad was in the lead and Opossum was walking point for the squad. He was a great point man. He was observant and cautious and never got lost. About an hour or so into the hump, an explosion rang out. Opossum was down. I could hear him screaming. I dreaded racing up to see what was left of him.

When I arrived, Lee was crouched around him and trying to pull him from a bomb crater that the blast had thrown him into. We pulled him to the trail and I yelled to form a perimeter and to call for a medi-vac chopper. Opossum was in shock. I sat on top of him slapping him wildly, yelling at him, "Opossum, wake up. Come on, man, open those eyes, you prick. Come on, man, hold on. Your bird is on the way. Hang with me, buddy!" He began to come out of shock and was thrashing in horrible pain. I surveyed his wounds. His legs appeared to be okay although peppered with the familiar holes caused by a mine exploding. His back, ass, legs, and the back of his arms were laden with holes, and blood was everywhere.

"Are my legs there, Dark. Don't bullshit me, man. Are my legs there?" He was struggling to rise up to see if indeed they were there. I helped him rise up so he could see for himself. Once he saw that they were there he was calmer although still in excruciating pain.

Doc ran up to administer aid to him and I held his hand to give him comfort. He gritted his teeth and held on until the chopper arrived. He was shaking and quivering from fear and anguish, wondering if he would live. I didn't show it, but I was wondering the same thing. The chopper dropped in, blowing the surrounding bush in the air, slapping us in the face as we loaded Opossum on the bird. He lifted off, and my prayers were with him.

Once Opossum was on his way to Da Nang, the terror of the moment set in. My anger grew into rage. I thought of all of the times we had spent together. I still heard his screams ringing in my ears. He was my friend and point man and these no-good bastards had taken him from me in the most cowardly way—the booby trap. They were weapons of cowards.

I looked at my hands and his blood was etched into my skin. I'd never forget his clammy hands, trembling and shaking with pain and fear, clutching mine as his blood seeped into my flesh. I vowed I'd get revenge, and I conceived a plan.

We pulled together and moved on and eventually settled into our night position. The next morning before the company moved out, I approached Lt. Maley and volunteered to set an ambush. The enemy knew well that American soldiers often left perfectly good C-rations and other gear behind when they left a position. I proposed that we drop off in the brush as the rest of the company moved out, wait for Charlie to show up scrounging for leftovers, and then kick their ass. The captain approved the deal. It would be my squad and an M60 machine gun squad who wanted to stay as well—for Opossum.

As Fox moved out, we dropped off in the bush and took up positions in the tall grass right next to the perimeter of our old camp. I felt a little squeamish after the company moved out, because if there were a hundred NVA waiting to move into our position I could be in a world of hurt. We sat silent and still for a few hours. Charlie was always cautious. Lee, who was sitting next to me, glanced over and pointed out in front of us. I raised up slightly and there in front of me, not more than ten meters way, was a NVA hardcore regular in full gear. His rifle was strapped on his shoulder. He wasn't prepared for what he was about to get.

I signaled to Lee to pass it on that I would start the ambush and everyone was to fire everything they had. If there was one NVA, there were probably many more that we couldn't see. I rose up slowly with my weapon wedged into my shoulder and sighted in on the soldier. I knew he was mine. I had him. He was looking down on the ground searching for C-rations and I was about to pull the trigger when he saw me, and he panicked. I saw his eyes widen with surprise; he knew he was about to die. I shot him in the back when he turned to run away and then opened up on the surrounding area on automatic. I saw him drop. Without thinking, I charged toward him and yelled for everyone to advance. Everyone was spraying the area and the M60 guys were laying everything low. If there were any more gooks out there, they were running the other way. We only received sporadic fire, and it soon subsided.

Cobb screamed out, "I see him and he is trying to get away."

I yelled, "Shoot the bastard," as I tried to catch up with him. I heard the rounds fly and then a large explosion rocked the elephant grass surrounding the scene. As I arrived, Cobb was on one knee holding his head. There was blood on his face. There lay the NVA, who was still twitching. He was face down. I walked up to him and coldly fired a round into the back of his head. That was for Opossum!

Then I realized what had happened. Cobb had fired a burst up the NVA's back, and when he shot, a frag that the NVA had on his ammo belt blew and hit Cobb in the forehead. That was Cobb's second Purple Heart, and that meant he was out of the bush.

When I rolled the gook over his face was literally gone. The rifle round had turned his face into a mish-mash of goo. We stripped the gook of all of his gear, taking his pack, rifle, and other possessions and then, as additional revenge, I took an ace of spades from a deck of cards, wrote "Don't mess with Fox 2/5 USMC" on it, and jammed it into the gooks face with a stick.

I recalled in boot camp when Gunny said that he had seen the enemy lying on the battlefield with his brains drying out in the sun and he had smelled rotting flesh. Now I understood. I never anticipated that I would be responsible for such a scene.

We picked up the gear and started to catch up with Fox. No one said a word on the hump back to the company position. Everyone was in shock from the killing. This was personal. It was murder anywhere else in the world, but today it was war.

Everyone was excited but afraid of the fury unleashed from within each of us. Each man was soul searching, trying to sort out his actions. I began to struggle with what I had done. It was a heinous part of me that I never knew lay deep inside. It scared me, and I think it scared the other marines who were with me that day. Had that really been me? Was I really capable of committing such an atrocious act to another human being? Or was the NVA just an animal?

Then I remembered the sticky, wet blood from Opossum's hand as his hand squeezed mine, as I held my friend, blown away by this enemy's cowardly, inhumane, and illegal booby traps that were meant to cripple and kill my fellow marines, and I refused to feel guilt for brutally killing my enemy. I felt like a battle-scarred wolf becoming immune to death. I thought of all of the nights when I was so scared that I couldn't breathe and the AK-47 rounds whizzing through my mind and the blast of the mines that blew my marine buddies away and watching my men squirm on the ground in pain, and I didn't care anymore. The NVA was responsible for the demons fighting within my gut while I was trying to maintain my sanity and not be a coward. My mind echoed with the haunting scream of "Corpsman up, corpsman up," and the unmistakable smell of burnt flesh, and I didn't give a damn about the son of a bitch that I killed. Did I go over the line? No doubt, but anyone who would viciously blow up my friend wasn't worth feeling guilt over. I'll let the marines who witnessed the horrible scene be the judge.

Once we returned to the perimeter, everyone crowded around to listen as we described the ambush to the lieutenant. An interpreter that was traveling with us started to read aloud the letters that were in the NVA's pack. It turned out that he was a squad leader, twenty years old, wounded once, and had just returned from the hospital in North Vietnam. He was from Hanoi and carried a picture of his girlfriend in his wallet. The description of the NVA matched my own.

After learning the guy's name and listening to the letters from his family, it hit me. Indeed, he was another human being. A few hours before, he was nothing to me. Now I thought of his eyes as they widened in fear, knowing that he was about to die. However, war is war, and people do things in the craziness of battle that they are not proud of. I wasn't proud of what I did and I am the one who must live with it. No one should have been treated the way that I treated that NVA soldier. He probably didn't want to be here fighting anymore than I did. I regretted the way I acted, but being thrown on the battlefield and watching the hideous events unfold before my eyes, as a twenty-year-old kid, inevitably a rage built inside me, as it did with every marine, and sometimes it spilled out uncontrollably.

What scared me most was knowing what I was capable of. I would never have imagined that I could behave the way that I did. But given the state of mind I was in, and placed in the same circumstances, with the horrors of war surrounding me, I'd respond the same way. Perhaps I went into a temporary state of insanity? I don't know.

One can't judge the actions that marines took according to the standards of a society at peace while living one's daily life back in the "world." We were living day to day with an enemy trying to kill us and we were trying to survive by killing them. We saw death often. Don't be quick to judge unless you've had the wet, sticky blood of a friend etched into your skin. And make no mistake—killing is brutal and there is nothing civilized about it.

Chapter 12

War is cruelty. There's no use trying to reform it, the crueler it is the sooner it will be over.

—William Tecumseh Sherman

We had humped all around the eastern half of Ga Noi Island and now we were to operate with the ARVN to sweep across the rest of the area, making our way back toward a small village called Cu Ban. We were to hump for five or six thousand meters until we met up with them to sweep for the NVA. The terrain was miserable to hump through. It consisted of marsh grass, tall elephant grass, knee-deep swampy areas, and heavily booby-trapped trails.

The monsoon was worse than ever and the continuous cloud cover made navigating difficult. In Vietnam, we guided ourselves by using notable landmarks, and when it rained and it was foggy with low-lying clouds, our landmarks could be easily confused. One hill looked a lot like another. We were pretty low, and then the bad news came.

Lt. Maley called the squad leaders together and told us that we would be moving at night. How many times did we have to go through a nighttime movement before these officers realized that it was suicide? Hadn't they learned anything? But what did I know? I had only lost half my squad at night. The only good news was that at least we didn't have point for the company. If we got hit, it would be someone else for a change.

If the intent of moving at night was to sneak up on the enemy, it was a joke. A hundred marines moving in a column cannot be quiet. A happy marine is a grumpy, complaining marine. Guys fell, stumbled, cursed when they fell in a hole full of marsh water, or slipped in the rain into a bomb crater. Quiet is not a word to describe a night movement of pissed off marines. A half-deaf VC could hear us coming from a mile away. Why risk hitting booby traps or getting ambushed at night? I just didn't get it.

We moved out and it took forever. Guys were getting separated from the man in front of them, so they would occasionally take the wrong trail and have to back up, which caused everyone behind them to stop, bunch up, and wonder what was going on. Occasionally we'd hear someone who was frustrated with the pace of the movement yell, "Hey, what the hell is going on up there?" Of course, they were quickly reprimanded, but we all had a good laugh knowing this movement was a fiasco. It was humping ten feet and bending over, trying to get relief from the weight on your back.

It wasn't funny anymore when we heard M16 fire and AK-47s answering. Then we heard explosions and saw flares in the air over the front of the column. We were powerless to do anything, since we were in single file, and trying to rush to the front of the column was impossible in the darkness. Lt. Maley got on the radio and tried to get his orders.

Lt. Maley called each squad leader to form a perimeter, spread out, and settle in for the night and be alert that the VC had hit Second Platoon hard and they were trying to get medivac choppers to respond. I doubted they could fly in tonight because of the cloud cover and rain, which was now falling hard. There was sporadic fire all night. The VC would run up to our positions, throw a satchel charge, or fire a few rounds into the perimeter without being detected in the dark. We returned fire in the direction of any movement in front of us. Sometimes we just fired our weapons for the hell of it just in case the gooks were even thinking about approaching our position. We got no confirmed kills.

Finally, when daylight arrived, we discovered the degree to which Second Platoon got hit. Paul Koonce, a lance corporal from my hometown, was severely wounded. He lost an arm and a leg and had severe head wounds. An 81 mm mortar spotter was killed, and many others were wounded. I was frustrated because I never fired a shot.

The next day we pulled together, loaded up our gear, and continued the hump to meet the ARVN. It was a long haul through the lowlands, but we finally arrived at the rendezvous location. When we arrived, we found the ARVN hanging in the hammocks under poncho hooches, listening to their radios, squatting next to their pots of stinking fishy crap they ate. Everyone smelled of the incense they burned constantly.

The ARVN cancelled the sweep because the weather was too bad. They didn't feel like humping in the rain. How typical—Americans were giving their lives and spilling their blood so the ARVN could hang around sleeping in their cozy hammocks! This was bullshit. We began flipping them out of their hammocks, laughing when they hit the ground jabbering their irritating language at us. Who cared? They were lucky that's all we did. I thought of Paul Koonce, who was wounded badly, and these bastards didn't care enough to hump in the rain. Now I disliked the ARVN almost as much as the NVA or VC and didn't trust them at all. I had no respect for these people—there was no way they would win this war without us; that was clear. These chicken-shit soldiers didn't deserve our precious blood.

That night movement changed my perception of the war and why we were here. We came in good faith to fight for America and to free Vietnam. Now we were doing the fighting and they were watching. It would have been funny if marines weren't dying and being crippled for life.

Our remaining days in Ga Noi got worse. It rained hard for four days straight without relief. All we could do was hunker down and try to stay dry, which was impossible. The choppers couldn't fly to bring us supplies, and our chow ran out. Our ammo was getting short as well, and for the first time since I came to Vietnam, I worried that if we got hit hard we might run out of firepower. If Charlie knew how bad it was; it would have been a perfect time for him to strike.

Four more days passed and guys were getting weak from not eating. I'd never been starved for four days before. An interesting thing happens. The first day your stomach growls and you hurt from being empty. Then after the second day, you notice that the pain is no worse, and then after that it almost subsides. But all we could think of was food. I thought about pizza, hamburgers, my mom's biscuits, and even those horrible beef and rocks C-rations that I disdained when I first arrived in country sounded wonderful. We chopped down a banana tree and boiled it, but after a few bites we threw up.

Finally, the weather broke, and the choppers dropped in with supplies. We feasted on those lousy rations as if they were the best New York sirloin we could imagine. We thought we would eat for hours, but after four days of no food, a few bites were all we could hold.

At last we were leaving Ga Noi, and good riddance! It had been a nightmare. I had been in country seven months now. January and February had been checked off my helmet.

♦   ♦   ♦

We learned that we would be going back to road security around Liberty Bridge. The good news was that during the day, we'd split up into small units along the road and provide security for the convoys. That part of the duty was a skate (easy). The bad news was that every night, we would move off the road and set up ambushes. It was a heavily booby trapped area, so we had to be very cautious wherever we moved.

The monsoon finally broke. We finally got relief from sleeping in the rain, and our gook sores began to heal. It was nice to wake up with your clothes dry and not soaking wet on one side. The sun finally dried up our feet.

We also enjoyed a tremendous luxury while guarding the road. We gave the convoy marines money and they would drop off Cokes and an occasional beer or two on their way back to An Hoa from Da Nang.

We also received plenty of fresh cigarettes, and real toilet paper—not that crummy stuff they had in C-rations. There was a standing joke that it didn't wipe your ass; it just cut you a new one. Occasionally a gook would come by to give haircuts and an occasional massage.

Vietnam was wearing me out. I was tired of being dirty all the time and crapping in a hole like a cat. I wanted a shower so bad. I dreamed of soaking in a big tub for as long as I wanted. I was sick of this chow. How many ways could you spice up beanie weenies? I hated the smell of Marine Corps cologne, the bug juice we mopped on every night to keep the little monsters from stinging us to death.

I no longer wanted others to look to me for leadership. It would be nice to worry only about myself for a change. What a great feeling it would be to no longer be responsible for other marines' lives. I was tired of getting paranoid when the evening arrived, knowing that the darkness was close and it was time for Charlie to hunt us again. I knew that if I ever made it home it would take a long time to enjoy the night again. It would be nice to be alone. I hadn't been alone since joining the marines. I longed for the day when I could lie in my own bed, under my fan, with the door closed, and just be by myself.

I thought about my buddy Bove and wondered if he was okay. By chance, one day while standing watch along the road, I saw the familiar cloud of dust from a convoy on the horizon. As it approached, I saw Bove, waving frantically, jumping up and down in the back of the flat-bed truck.

"Hey, Dark," he screamed. "I'm going on R&R and I'll get a little bit for you."

He shot me the bird and disappeared in a cloud of dust. I was relieved to see that he was okay. It would be good to shoot the bull with him again. We'd made plans for when we got back to the world. Now that our time was getting short, I began to believe that we would get the opportunity to carry them out.

One night we set up a nighttime observation post just off the road, only about five hundred meters from the platoon. Starkey and three other guys came along. The area didn't seem "hot," so I believed that five guys would be enough firepower if we hit the shit. Besides, we weren't setting an ambush; we were just watching for movement.

Each of us stood watch for an hour, rotating throughout the night. During my watch, I observed a village about three hundred meters away. The full moon made it easy to detect movement, and I kept seeing figures moving in single file. There was no way villagers would be moving about at night. I opened up on the village and everyone started firing. We started getting return fire, and Cole caught a round in his arm. He said he was okay and we kept up the heat.

I radioed to the lieutenant that we needed artillery, called in the coordinates, and asked for a "Willy Peter round" (white phosphorous). Then I called for effective fire. The rounds dropped, yet the firing from the enemy remained intense.

"Lieutenant, I need additional support. The gooks must be dug in."

I guess Maley could hear the anxiousness in my voice. "We have Spooky coming your way," he said. Now we would see a show. Spooky was a converted DC-3 equipped with mini-guns capable of literally showering the enemy with hundreds of thousands of rounds. When he fired the tracer rounds, which were every sixth round, they looked like a red snake coming from heaven, sweeping across the ground. The barrage went on for what seemed like an hour, and then all was quiet.

We bandaged up Cole, and he said he could wait to catch a chopper in the morning rather than risk a night medivac. The next morning he caught his bird to Da Nang and the captain asked us to sweep the village to find the dead NVA.

We found nothing. No bodies. The captain was pissed. In his opinion, we had just wasted precious Marine Corps firepower for nothing. I'm not sure Cole agreed with his summation, but I felt sorry for Lt. Maley, because I'm sure he got his ass chewed as well. We all felt kind of bad that we didn't kill the NVA, but they were very good about hauling the wounded and dead off the battlefield, so just because they weren't lying on the ground everywhere didn't mean that we didn't inflict great damage on them.

Two days later, Lt. Maley called me to his hooch. As I walked up, he smiled and stretched out his hand. "Congratulations, Dark. I just heard from the rear." He was grinning widely now. "Intelligence confirmed that we stopped a hundred or so NVA trying to cross the river behind that village last night. If we had not stopped them, they might well have overrun our position. I'm recommending you for a Bronze Star."

One minute I was a goat, and now I was a hero. I never got my Bronze Star. I guess when it got up to the captain for his approval he couldn't get over the fact that we didn't have a body count. I didn't really care. Cole was all right, and that's all that mattered to me.

◆   ◆   ◆

I reached a dangerous point in my tour of Nam. I was getting a little more "out there," kind of doing crazy stuff. One night I was on watch using a starlight scope, which enabled us to see at night. I was looking down the road. We were set up in an ambush right off the road, not more than fifty meters. As I watched the road, I saw movement. It was definitely a soldier, but I couldn't tell if he was friendly or not. I got on the radio and asked if it were possible that friendly forces were operating in the same area. The answer was negative. As I expected, a group of marines would never move down an open road at night.

"Starkey," I whispered, "let the lieutenant know that we have movement on the road and we are going to creep up along side of the road and open up when they get in range." He nodded and disappeared into the bush and soon returned. The M60 machine gun squad didn't want to get left out, so off we went to slip up on the VC moving straight at us. The only problem was that I forgot the starlight scope, and now I didn't have a clue where the gooks were. For all I knew, they could have left the road and been right in front of us.

I couldn't stand it anymore. I lined everyone up along the road and passed the word that when I started firing, follow suit and let them have it. Then we started firing. As soon as we did, green tracers started flying back at us, revealing that it was definitely the enemy. Because of my poor planning, we had no real cover. I rolled into a shallow ditch next to the road on my back as the tracers flew over my belly. I tried to press harder into the dirt. The tracers were so close that I swear I felt the heat, not much different that when I got caught in the river ambush. We all went a little wild and started screaming and yelling, throwing frags and firing our weapons while we hid in the ditch.

Starkey screamed at me, "Great idea, Dark. How long did you think about this one? I'm gonna get my dick shot off. Remind me to kick your ass if I live through this." We laughed and screamed, watching the rounds shoot across our chests, going crazy and entering that familiar twilight zone of battle.

When the firing stopped, no one was wounded, so we went back to the platoon laughing and cutting up, much to Lt. Maley's dismay. He didn't find it as funny as we did. It was stupid, but we released a lot of tension.

I knew after that night that I'd better be careful for the rest of my tour or I'd do something crazy and get blown away.

Chapter 13

Never give in—never, never, never, never, in nothing great or small, large or petty, never give in except to convictions of honor and good sense. Never yield to force; never yield to the apparently overwhelming might of the enemy.

—Sir Winston Churchill

A complete shocker came down from the rear. Every marine with nine months in country would be leaving the bush. President Nixon was pulling out the marines. I had eight months and three weeks in country. I wouldn't be leaving. I thought about Bove, because he wouldn't be leaving either, and I bet he was pissed. It was hard to watch all my buddies leaving the field. I lost several guys from my squad who had more time in country than me, and all the other squad leaders were leaving. All the experienced marines in the bush were rotating, and I felt really insecure. The only good news was that I became platoon sergeant and got meritoriously combat promoted to corporal; the bad news was that now I had more responsibility.

One thing for sure—the VC weren't pulling out of Vietnam. They were finding new ways to kill marines. The VC learned how to take an unexploded bomb, lean it on a paddy dike near a marine position, pack a charge under the bomb, set it off, and hurl it into the perimeter. The prospect of a five-hundred-pound bomb being hurled into our position at night was disturbing. We stopped calling our movements "operations," even though they were. The politicians wanted to present a more passive approach to the war while at the bargaining table in Paris.

The less time I had left in the bush, the more paranoid I got. I thought I was about to crack. I even tried faking a wound, which was stupid.

"Nice try, dumbass," Doc said. I was humiliated just thinking about it. I already had one Purple Heart and, one more would get me out of the bush, but I knew I'd never go through with it. I wouldn't have been able to live with myself if I had carried that out. Your mind can play havoc with you in such circumstances. If I'd had one more week in country, I would have met the nine-month requirement and would have left the bush and been able to put Vietnam behind me. When I thought about walking point in the Arizona into the village where Donnie had been killed, racing into enemy fire on Charlie Ridge, volunteering to set an ambush to get even for Opossum, and killing twenty NVA and capturing twenty-eight others next to the river that fateful day next to the Arizona, I knew that I was no coward. I'd stick it out no matter what and go home when my time was up, honorably. If I was killed now, well, I'd go out proudly.

Just when I thought things couldn't get any worse, I received a godsend. I was to report to the rear in An Hoa as the NCOIC (noncommissioned officer in charge) of the rear. It was a skate, and I'd be out of the bush! A week earlier I was ready to do anything to get out of the bush, and now that I was going honorably. I understood the ambivalence of leaving my buddies in the bush. It was as if I was deserting them. But that's life in the military, particularly during war. Relationships are constantly changing. Guys you had coffee with in the morning were gone in an instant, blown away by the enemy. Over and over I had suffered loneliness and loss.

But I was hauling my ass out of the bush. I promised to write and send the guys some chow from the rear. I caught a convoy back to An Hoa, unable to believe I had made it out of the bush alive. If I could survive just a few months in the rear, the odds of which were good, then I would make it home.

I actually thought that there was a good chance I'd be there only a few weeks, meet the nine-month requirement, and then leave Nam early, but Nixon screwed that up when he decided to go into Cambodia and all early rotations were cancelled. I would be in Vietnam for my entire tour. But at least I'd be in the rear. My responsibilities consisted of assigning bunker watch and assigning other duties to boots joining the company or old salts leaving. I didn't have to stand bunker watch, although I checked on the guys to make sure they weren't sleeping.

Things were going well until our new first sergeant, Smith, called me into the office.

"Corporal Dark, did you know a Sergeant Boyd?" He asked, wondering why he referred to him in the past tense.

"Yeah, first sergeant. Why?" I said curiously.

"I need you to go to Da Nang to identify his body. He got blown away yesterday. Apparently he sat down to take a break while on a hump and hit a mine. His dog tags must have been blown off; they need someone to be sure that it's him." He scribbled out my orders and handed them to me. "Chopper leaves in about an hour. Be there."

With a heavy heart, I loaded on to the bird to Da Nang. I wished it were taking me out of this shithole of a country. I couldn't imagine a worse mission. I had known Boyd. What a great guy he was. He was a sergeant and, like me, he hadn't had enough time in country to leave, so he had to remain in the bush. He had bushy hair and a big moustache to match. Now he was gone.

When I arrived at the hospital, I was directed to the morgue, then into a large freezer, much like the ones in grocery stores where the meat is hung. On the wall there were shelves and on the shelves bodies in black bags were stacked on top of one another.

The duty marine walked over to the bag with Boyd's tag on it and unzipped it. Boyd still had blood on his face. His brown hair was dark brown now from the dried blood. His head was turned toward the wall of the freezer.

"I can't see his face," I said.

The duty marine reached out, grabbed Boyd's jaw, and twisted his face toward me. I pushed the marine back and screamed at him, "Get your hands off him, man. He is my friend. Don't you have more respect than that?" I stared him down and would have fought him if he took one step toward me. The rage was swirling inside, and I cried. This was my friend, and he lay on that shelf like a side of beef—and no one cared.

I stepped back and said, "Yeah, it's Boyd. Give me the paper to sign." I reached out and witnessed that it was my friend. In disgust, I turned and headed back to the chopper pad, reluctantly returning to An Hoa. Boyd served America honorably. He was a good marine. I was saddened to think of his family and how they were waiting for their son to return in one of those silver caskets that I saw when arriving in Vietnam almost a year earlier. My eyes filled with tears thinking about Boyd. He was going home. I couldn't get the image of his face—cold, twisted, blue, and ravaged from war—out of my head. He looked so much older than his early twenties. I guess we all looked older than our age. War does that to youth. You arrived in Vietnam a kid and left an old man, having witnessed things no kid should see.

A few days passed and before I could get the memory of Boyd out of my mind, I was standing next to my hooch, and a guy from Echo Company walked over to me.

"You were Bove's buddy, weren't you?"

Bove was dead. I could tell from the way the marine said it. Still, I forced myself to ask, with some hope in my voice, "Is he okay?"

"He stepped on a booby trap. A mortar round. He was on patrol," he answered. "They flew him to Da Nang and he fought off death for three days, but he died. He was messed up bad. I think he lost an arm and a leg. I thought that you would want to know." He turned and walked away.

Had I been in Da Nang at the same time Bove was in the hospital? Maybe I could have been there for him. I gazed over the barbed wire that surrounded that lousy compound in that worthless pigsty of a country. My best friend, Bove, was dead. He died just as he thought he would. I pictured him standing in front of me, that strong, arrogant athlete of a man, a true marine in every sense, my best friend. He was as strong as an ox, defiant, proud, tough, and so full of life. Nothing could ever get him down. Every time I got dejected, he had been there to cheer me up. Now he was gone at age twenty. I could imagine the scene: him lying in the dirt, wounded and alone, while his buddies tried to save his life while the chopper raced him to Da Nang, where the docs circled around him trying to give him every chance to survive. God, I wish I had been there for him. I could have held his hand, as I held Opossum's and comforted him. I could have felt him shake, and with my hand in his he would have known that his friend cared. But I wasn't there for him. If only someone had told me before it was too late.

Maybe it was best that he died. He was so proud. I doubt that Bove would have been able to stand being bound in a wheelchair. His strong arm that he used to throw out runners trying to steal second base was gone. One of his muscular legs that he marched on while leading his marine platoon at Parris Island was gone. I couldn't believe that he was dead. How cruel to last this long and get killed with so little time left. How could God have taken this young marine?

Bitterness filled my heart. I was angry at everyone and felt like going back to the bush to kill anything that moved. I raced back to my hooch and loaded my gear and told the first sergeant that I wanted to go back to the bush. I felt the same rage that came spilling out when Opossum got blown away, and now I would get even.

I guess the first sergeant saw the rage, as he made me sit down for an hour and talked to me, calming me down. Then he insisted that I visit the chaplain for counseling, and finally I realized that the last thing Bove would have wanted me to do was go back to the bush.

Then I thought about the pledge. How could I face his mother and brother? There was no way I could face them. I'd rather face a hundred NVA than watch his mother cry. I knew I would have to deal with this eventually, but for now I just wept for my friend. The world lost a trea-sure the day that Harmon Bove was killed. He was a good man, a real marine, and he fought like it. He was the epitome of strength and per-sonal dignity. I was proud to have known him, and it was an honor to serve with him and to be a small part of his life. He was my friend and I loved him. And like so many other things about Vietnam, his death was tragic. He'd live in my heart always.

I wrote a letter home:

March 5, 1970

Dear Mom,

Bove is dead. He was blown away by a booby trap and the world won't be the same without him. He was a brother that I never had. He died a marine fighting in Vietnam for all of the lousy and lazy civilians back in the world, sitting on their couches, drinking their beers. Too many good marines have died. I've learned that death has no prejudice. I had a bet that we would be out of here by the end of February. I lost and so did Bove.

Love, Gene

For the rest of my tour I just went through the motions. I was tired of the struggles of war. I was burnt out with glory and pride for the corps. I would do my job and I would remain vigilant, but my heart ached and mentally I was shot.

A few new boots joined Fox and I assigned them to bunker duty. That night when I checked to see if they were awake, I walked up behind the bunker I caught one of the boots smoking. I chewed him out and told him that if he had done that in the bush he would have gotten his ass beat. I told him not to do it again, and as I walked of he said, "Hey, Corporal, when you get back to the world are you going to tell your war stories of how you walked the line in the rear?" Then laughed, proud of himself.

I walked over to him and said, "Hey, shitbird, do something for me. When you get to the field, ask any of those guys in the field about me." Then I got right in his face, as Gunny had done to me in boot camp. "Try to survive in the bush as long as I did—and by the way, let's see how you like standing watch by yourself tonight." I turned to the other guys on the bunker duty and said, "I better not catch either one of you standing his watch, and I will be back to check."

After everything I'd been through, for a boot to pop off like that pissed me off. I could only imagine what T-Byrd would have done to this guy.

Vietnam was full of irony. The boot was assigned to my old squad, which Lee ran now. He was killed in action after just a few days in the bush. Lee told me that he was shot when he raised his arm to take a drink from his canteen. Death took the good guys and the cocky boots. Death didn't discriminate.

I finally got my orders on June 26, 1970, to sky out of this dump.

Chapter 14

I took my last steps to the chopper waiting on the pad that would fly me out of An Hoa for the last time and take me to Da Nang where I'd catch my freedom bird home. Until I got on the chopper, I was convinced that Charlie would drop a mortar round right on top of my ass at the very last minute, just to get even, and when the artillery just behind me fired a volley of rounds, I almost had heart failure. I remembered when the sergeant that guided us to An Hoa had a good laugh when I dove to the ground thinking that the artillery was incoming. I'd come a long way since then, but it still scared the crap out of me.

We lifted off the LZ and as An Hoa disappeared behind me, I strained to see if I could find my company in the bush below. I surveyed the landscape below but couldn't see them. The landscape hadn't changed at all. Just a few more bomb craters and my marine buddies were still down there in the bush, humping around, setting off booby traps, sleeping in the rain, staring into the dark night, just trying to survive, all while Charlie was still humping mortar rounds from Hanoi trying to blow them away.

I spent an entire year of my life in Vietnam playing this deadly game, and what difference had I made? I'd given so much and gone through so much, and what had I really accomplished? The earth was pitted with bomb craters that my buddies had to drink from occasionally while they prayed every night for God to spare them for one more day.

I flew over all the areas that I had called home for the past year—the Arizona, Ga Noi, Phu Lac, the mountains where we pulled Operation

Durham Peak, the many rivers where I came so close to dying. I even saw Hill 65 and Charlie Ridge in the distance and wondered how many marines would meet their fate in those God-forsaken places today. The proud and defiant marines were so young, too young to be dying such horrible deaths in this desolate place on the battlefield.

Vietnam wasn't unique when it came to young men dying for their country. History is riddled with such places: Guadalcanal, Iwo Jima, Dunkirk, Normandy, Tripoli, and endless other battlefields throughout time. The battlefields are all the same. Young men give their lives in battle. The battlefield is a solemn, ghostly place, a silent graveyard for the brave.

No matter what happened to this desolate land in the coming years, the souls of the young dead warriors and their precious spent blood and guts mixed in to the mud would forever scream out. *Remember what happened here; never forget. Please, God, don't forget.*

As I flew over Vietnam for the last time, I remembered the faces of all who were lost and said a prayer for their souls. I swore I'd never forget their faces. I'd never seen such bravery, known such fear, or cried such lonesome tears for my fallen friends. I prayed for the ones remaining and asked God to guide their steps, to wrap his arms around them with love and send the angels of mercy who often protected me, to protect them and lift them up when they needed it most. That was my prayer. I would miss those brave marines, and I knew I would never have as much compassion for another human as those mean-ass sons of bitches, those young marines that I served with in battle. God, I loved them, and they would occupy my memories and my broken heart for the rest of my life.

How long would I think about the endless rain and the gook sores, the hot, relentless sun baking our young bodies, the sounds of battle? I knew that Vietnam was etched deeply in my psyche, more deeply than I could even imagine. It would take a long time to purge the memories, if I ever could. But I was finally on my way home. I had cheated death.

I was relieved to get to Da Nang and I immediately looked up Doc Seeley. He was a corpsman who I served with and who I most admired. He was in the navy, but he was a marine to me. He went on ambushes and fought beside us, even though he wasn't supposed to. I saw him sacrifice his own safety for a fallen marine. He and I had been through some tough times, and for a corpsman he was one tough, crazy guy. He was in Da Nang now, and I wanted to make sure no more marines from Fox 2/5 had been hit lately. I had a beer with him and we hugged as I left for the base where my freedom bird was waiting for me.

I remembered the times that I'd lay on my poncho in the bush, day-dreaming, looking skyward in a moment of peace and quiet, and I'd see the jet stream of a plane tens of thousands of feet above, and think what I wouldn't give to be on that bird, no matter where it was going, because anywhere had to be better than where I was trapped. Now it was my turn to leave.

Everyone was silent as we taxied down the runway, and when we lifted off and went into a steep climb, a spontaneous roar burst from the cabin. Everyone on that bird was thinking the same thing: that we had survived and we were on our way home. Home—what a sweet word. Was it really possible that I had made it?

◆   ◆   ◆

As the shoreline of Vietnam drifted past my window thousands of feet below, I realized how innocent I had been when I arrived in Vietnam and how much I had learned about life, war, and how cruel it could really be. I was a naive kid of just nineteen when I joined the marines. I thought that I could just pop over here to play war for a year, like some cavalier romantic, and then live the rest of my life immune from the horrible memories of battle. I knew now that memories of war would be embedded in my mind and that I would recall them every day, forever.

As a kid, I used to lay on a bed of pine straw in my backyard on a cool autumn day and contemplate what life had in store for me. I often felt lonely and lost, overwhelmed by the expectations others had for me. But at least the world seemed a secure place, full of fun and adventure. Now I knew the world as an ugly place full of heartache, pain, and horror. Now I had learned what the real world was like.

The young always fight the battles, but I felt so old now. Is it true that only a year had passed? I laughed inside when I thought about how, as a stupid kid just out of high school, I'd grown bored with life and grown tired of fitting the mold, always doing the right thing, and so joined the marines. For the past year, while most kids were experiencing the excitement of going to college and preparing for their future, I'd been dealing with the grief, fear, loneliness, and the heartache of war. I'd no doubt become a stronger person because of my ordeal, but it saddened me to think that innocence had been ripped from my heart at the tender age of nineteen. Innocence should be lost slowly and given up grudgingly. Only when one is no longer a child should he be subjected to the real, cruel, unforgiving world that we live in. As a young teen I had been run through boot camp, pumped with thoughts of invincibility, and molded into a marine. They gave me a rifle and twenty magazines of ammo and then dropped me on the battlefield to try to survive. And let there be no doubt—I was just the kind of kid that America needed on the battlefield, because I had nothing to lose. Once I saw a few marines wounded and felt the pangs of war, I killed without hesitation. I let it all hang out. Once I realized that it was a game of kill or be killed, America gave birth to a true soldier. The marines quickly made me a killer, molded from a kid. I became cold, callused, calculating, fine-tuned, alert, mean, and relentless. The marines did a good job, and they knew that if I didn't quickly succumb to that weird craziness, I wouldn't survive the rigors of war or protect my fellow marines. If I hadn't become an animal when I came face to face with the enemy, walking the line of insanity, I might have hesitated. Had I done so, I might have died, and if enough marines died, America would lose. America doesn't like to lose.

The enemy that I fought was tough as nails. Based upon my experience in the bush, I concluded that the Viet Cong had no morals and he did not care about right or wrong. He was born into poverty, deep in the mountains in a primitive world. The peasants just tried to survive from one pointless day to the next. If he made it to ten years old, he would have already cheated death many times. I doubt that he understood what freedom was and had no clue about government, let alone democracy or communism.

My enemy violated every honorable rule of war. I determined that war by rules was bullshit. If your country asks you to survive on the battlefield, then you throw out the rules. My enemy stuffed grenades into the pockets of thirteen-year-old kids and instructed them to hurl them at marines knowing that young soldiers had a soft spot for kids. The NVA set booby traps not just to kill marines but to severely wound them. A wounded marine was a marine off the battlefield. My enemy humped hundreds of miles just to deliver a bag of rice to his fellow soldiers. These people didn't seem to cherish life as we did. Lives seemed expendable. So why would they care about rules? The Viet Cong were true killers, and the enemy would cut your throat in a second if given the opportunity. He could be your buddy in the day and try to slip his knife between your ribs at night.

But even the so-called good guys, the South Vietnamese, didn't respect the life of their own countrymen. I recalled when we were set up on road security by Liberty Bridge. A platoon of ARVN moved into my position and starting shooting at kids perched on their water buffaloes just to sight in their rifles. I ran them off before anyone was wounded, but what did their actions say about how they felt about the sanctity of life? If they didn't care about the very people we were trying to protect, what was this war all about? That day had been an eye-opening experience for me. I learned that few other countries valued life and freedom as Americans do.

Vietnam taught me that people in a position of authority can't always be trusted and that I should never depend on anyone else to save my ass. I was alone in this world. I learned that you should never assume anything in life. A single wrong assumption could spell death. I also learned that the slightest hesitation could get you blown away. I had to always be alert. I'd live the rest of my life giving one hundred percent. I'd never be a shitbird, and I would expect the same from those who surrounded me.

I learned excuses are for the weak. "Excuses are like assholes," Gunny would say. "Everyone has one." Excuses were for the shitbirds who weren't man enough to admit their mistakes and go on with life. Hey, pick yourself up, admit that you were wrong, and go on. I wouldn't wallow in self-pity about anything.

I learned that life is so precious. It is regarded as blessed and sacred. I learned that everything in life took planning and hard work. Anything done haphazardly was unacceptable. The person who could out-think, out-hustle, and out-plan the enemy would win.

Finally, Vietnam taught me that nothing in life is fair. Nothing! And no one cares about being fair. Man is cruel and the world was raw. No one gave a rat's ass about your feelings. I wouldn't kid myself: life was a war, and I wouldn't be a loser. I'd win my war of life.

I would become an island, a rock. I'd separate myself from the world and never allow myself to feel pain or sorrow again. Never again would I cry!

War exposed me to the dark side of life, leaving memories that would tug at my heart forever. Everything in life would remind me of war. Civilians would never understand; they could simply switch the television off when the sights and sounds of battle made them uncomfortable. What did they know? It was just another war in a far-off country, and besides, it didn't affect their lives. But I could never turn it off. I was leaving Vietnam airspace, but I knew that I would never leave the memories of war.

I closed my eyes and they filled with tears of joy, then sadness as I again recalled the faces of those who should have been on the plane with me but hadn't made it. Every war is won by the boots, the grunts on the ground. Until soldiers square off fighting each other, one-on-one, wars are not won. After thousands of years of war, nothing had changed. It was 1970 and men still squared off against one another, hunting each other, each stalking and searching out his prey and brutally unleashing his weapon on his victim. He stared down the rifle sight and whispered to himself, "I have found you at last, and now you will die."

Since going to the bush with my unit in July 1969, I had known many brave marines who served and died on the battlefield with Fox 2/5. They already had their plane ride home:

2nd LT Albert Benson	7/6/69
CPL Michael Lewis	8/15/69
PFC Cliff Gibson	8/16/69
LCPL David Hartogh	9/7/69
PFC Larry Robillard	9/7/69
PFC Donnie Clough	9/9/69
SGT Albert Wright	10/19/69
LCPL Ronald Spence	11/28/69
LCPL Warren Ferguson	2/20/70
SGT John Boyd	3/15/70
PFC William Brooks	3/17/70
Corpsman George Cuthbert	3/29/70
SGT Ramon Moya	5/12/70
LCPL Arden Kersey	6/13/70
CPL William Arthur	6/19/70
LCPL John Brown	6/19/70
CPL Harmon Bove, Echo Co. 2/5	3/5/70

In addition to marines who were killed, I knew many more who had been wounded, busted up, and sent home to mend their broken bodies and minds. When I arrived in Da Nang, out of thirty-five marines that I arrived in Vietnam with who should have rotated when I did, only four of us were left, and all but one had a Purple Heart.

I was so fortunate to be alive. Why had I survived? Was I faster, smarter, or tougher than the other marines? Of course not; in fact, the opposite was probably true. Was it just fate? I felt guilty that so many braver men than me had died. Every soldier who ever fought a war feels the same way. Ask him and he will tell you about the guilt that he carries deep down inside for surviving when so many others died. I was so proud of these fallen marines. They had answered when their country called and had displayed incredible valor in the darkest of times. They mustered up smiles when circumstances were most difficult. When they had every excuse to quit, they strapped on their gear and pressed on like the true men they were. I felt proud to be a marine. Not the rah-rah crap of boot camp, but the pride of being battle-tested tough, never quitting, never giving up, and never running away. The marines taught me to survive war, and I had the comfort of knowing that I'd been faithful to my fellow marines.

I discovered that there was no glory in war. Why did the politicians glorify battle? I saw no glory. One thing for certain: if all of the politicians had served on the battlefield, watched their buddies die, felt the heat of napalm being dropped from the fighter jets as the tumbling bombs rolled across the jungle and then heard the screams of the enemy—if they had experienced war firsthand—I'm sure they wouldn't be so quick to send young men into battle. Death and fear change a person's view of war. Until you get a little blood on your hands, the real essence of war never sinks into your soul. One must understand what it's like to survive war, to fight and kill the enemy, before he can really appreciate the necessity of avoiding war at almost any cost.

Often, the reasons why wars are fought have nothing to do with glory, but there is nobility in fighting in an "American uniform" with other brave soldiers. There is honor on the battlefield, because on the testing ground of death and destruction, one finds out what lives deep inside real Americans, and it's magnificent.

Many guys hid when America called. The politicians argue and pound their fists on the grand podium in the Congress, fighting the war of words while they send the young soldiers to do their bidding on the field of war, to kill or be killed. What is it about man that makes it impossible to shake the violence and hate that churns within his heart and motivates him to kill another? I knew now that it is man's evil nature that manifests itself in the form of war. How else could I have behaved so evilly?

As Senator George McGovern said, "It doesn't require any particular bravery to stand on the floor of the Senate and urge our boys in Vietnam to fight harder, and if this war mushrooms into a major conflict and a hundred thousand young Americans are killed, it won't be U.S. Senators who die. It will be American soldiers who are too young to qualify for the Senate."

The government trains the soldiers, pumping their minds full of visions of invincibility and hatred of the enemy, teaching them to kill viciously and without mercy, in the name of God, country, honor, and duty. However, the politicians weren't the ones sitting on watch during a monsoon downpour or squeezing their rifle while walking point into the enemy's lair. I discovered that once on the battlefield, all that "rah-rah" politicians speak was bullshit. All that mattered was that if you didn't fight, you died. It became a game of him or you. So we fought until we died or the enemy died. We fought until it was time to go home. Others decide the reasons for going to war; when you are on the battlefield, it's just survival. Why you fought, sadly, is a moot point.

And marines weren't a bunch of hopheads running around killing babies either. The innocent were killed in war. People got killed who shouldn't have been, but I can honestly say I never saw the innocent murdered.

The marines that I served with did not use drugs on the battlefield. That doesn't mean they were boy scouts, but I know that in my squad, in the bush, it wasn't tolerated. I never did drugs for one minute in Vietnam, and neither did most other marines.

As Vietnam drifted off the horizon, disappearing into the past, I turned my thoughts to America. I was going home. I couldn't wait to see that familiar brown haze of Los Angeles, which was the last thing I had seen over a year ago when I was leaving America heading to Vietnam. When it appeared on the horizon, my heart leapt with joy and excitement. Smog never looked so good!

◆   ◆   ◆

After a few anxious days at Camp Pendleton, California, I was honorably discharged. I wore my uniform proudly, displaying the ribbons I had earned in battle. I carried my discharge papers tightly, not really believing that my time in the corps was done.

The first sergeant had tried to talk me in to re-enlisting right before I left Vietnam. I laughed, thinking that asking a marine to re-enlist when he had just survived fighting for his life was probably not the most opportune time. I was proud of what he wrote on the sheet, however: "Corporal Dark is an outstanding marine, who did his job to the best of his ability."

I couldn't have asked for more from anyone in the Marine Corps. It meant more to me than any medal that I could have won. To do a good job was all that I expected of myself. My Grandfather Dark had been right when he advised my father how important it was to do a good job no matter what you did in life. He knew that even if nobody noticed, if you knew in your heart that you did the best that you could do, that's what mattered. I was proud to have been a marine. Now I was going home and as I boarded the civilian aircraft, I still couldn't believe that it was true. I would sleep in my own bed tonight.

The flight attendants rolled their service cart down the aisle and I smelled the food. Even if it was airline food, I was looking forward to it. I sat in my uniform loving life, thinking about home and the big, warm hug I would get from my family. It had been a long time since I felt the warmth of love.

The stewardess handed a meal to the guy to my right, then looked at me and said, "I'm sorry, but we were overbooked, and since you are flying military standby, we won't be able to feed you. I have some peanuts if you like."

I wouldn't get a meal? Peanuts?

I knew that the guy next to me heard the comment, but he never looked up. He sat there reading his *Wall Street Journal* and never stopped feeding his face.

I churned inside. What had just happened? Didn't they know that I just left the battlefield? My friends were killed and maimed while fighting for them! Didn't they know that? Surely they could see the ribbons on my uniform. Did they mean nothing? I wouldn't get a lousy airline meal? Could it be true that no one on this plane cared enough to say, "Hey, marine, thanks for your service. Here, take my meal." There is no way that I would have accepted it, but it would have meant so much if just one person had offered.

I don't know why, but I remembered the list of marines who died, and my friend Bove, and feeling the sticky blood on my hands once I loaded Opossum on to the medivac chopper, and I thought, no one cared!

Not getting that meal on the plane was a fitting end to my service and summed up how I felt when returning home. I didn't care about parades or long, drawn-out speeches mumbled by politicians, by the very phonies who sent me to war in the first place. All I wanted was a word of encouragement, even a simple, "Thank you, marine."

How many years of bitterness would a kind word have erased? It was a sad commentary. My heart was heavy.

I'm sorry to say it, but it was true that evidently no one really cared about the medals on my chest or the great personal cost that it took to earn them. I decided at that moment that if America didn't care, then neither did I. Once I got home I took my medals and threw them in an old envelope and tossed my uniforms into a Salvation Army dumpster.

Chapter 15

War should belong to the tragic past, to history: It should find no place on humanity's agenda for the future.

—Pope John Paul II (Karol Josef Wojtyła)

Had America changed so much in the year that I was gone, or had I changed? I slept in the secure refuge of my room tucked between the clean, cold sheets on my soft, dry bed, which I had dreamed of while laying in the mud and being soaked from the monsoon rain. I listened to my fan blow the cool breeze on my face while I stared at the ceiling, thinking about my buddies in Vietnam. Every time I walked by the refrigerator, I'd open the door just to feel the coolness escape and occasionally take a drink of cold, perfectly clear water just because it was there. I thought about my fellow marines, still in the jungle or humping through the booby-trapped foothills, their gear rubbing their backs raw as they struggled to reach down and fill their canteens from a stinking water well in a lousy village.

When night fell it bothered me to walk outside by myself. I still cupped my hands around a cigarette so Charlie wouldn't see the glow. While in Vietnam I had so looked forward to being by myself, being alone with no responsibility, yet now I was uneasy and insecure. I felt vulnerable and defenseless, like an unprotected child. I had been a marine in the midst of war, so why was being alone such a spooky feeling?

Hardly a moment went by when I didn't think about my men whom I'd left behind in the bush. I should have been back there fighting with them. The feeling quickly subsided, because I knew there was no way I would consider such a thing, but the sense of desertion was there. The brotherhood of the marines was hard to break.

We had been discharged as fast as possible, and had the government taken a little time to indoctrinate us back into society, the fear, guilt, and alienation we felt could have been reduced.

I never knew it, but Doug had an interesting time in the marines. He had been assigned stateside as a typist, but after an altercation with another marine (whom he beat senseless), he was busted to private and then shipped him off to Vietnam. He served in Golf Company 2/5 and was wounded in an ambush and awarded the Bronze Star for valor. I wouldn't have expected less from Doug. I went to look him up.

We visited for a while, but I quickly realized that there was tremendous tension between Doug and his wife. I left quickly. I heard that after a few weeks of trying to make the marriage work, they gave up and his wife filed for divorce. Doug was never the same after that ambush. I never see him anymore.

Next I went to see Paul Koonce, who was from my hometown and had been severely wounded that night in Go Noi. He lost an arm and a leg at the knee. I dreaded going to visit him, but I had to do it. I found him in a smoke-filled trailer tucked into the woods on the outskirts of town. He hadn't been fitted with an artificial leg, so he sat in a wheelchair. A hook replaced the once-strong arm blown away that night in Nam. Scars ran down his face like melted wax down a candle, yet he smiled when I walked through the door. We hugged for a long time and shared tears for a while. There were unspoken emotions as we looked at one another, each of us knowing what the other was thinking. Then I realized that we had nothing in common anymore except the dreary, hate-filled days of Vietnam. We tried to shoot the bull for a while, but I found an excuse to leave as fast as I could. It was just too painful to see him slumped in that prison of a wheelchair. We promised to stay in touch, but I'd never called him again. Years later, when he died, I saw his obituary in the paper and noted where he would be laid to rest. I watched from a distance. I couldn't bring myself to be by his side.

Then something wonderful happened. I fell in love with my future wife, Nettie. Without her love I don't know how I would have made it through my tough times. She is the sweetest, most loving person in the world, and without her love I would not be the man that I am today.

The war still raged inside me, and I knew that I was such a different person from the kid who had left for Vietnam just a few years before. I dreamed often of Opossum's blood on my hands. Only a few other marines knew what I was capable of, having killed with these hands. I'd never tell Nettie of the things that I'd done. She could never love someone who had performed such hideous acts.

I tried to put the war behind me. I tried to forget the past, let the memories fade, gather dust, and blow away, but they never did. I couldn't do anything about what had happened to me. I couldn't recall the bullet that slammed into the NVA soldier that I killed, nor could I remove the stick I that I drove with rage into his face. I couldn't forget standing on the riverbank shooting VC like shadows in the water. By now, they were all just dust blowing through the tall elephant grass of Vietnam. But I still see the NVA's eyes forever—the haunting eyes of someone who was about to die. The ghostly, gray, dead face of my enemy giving testimony of my victory over him.

Over the years, I questioned what war meant to me on a personal level. I had been constantly challenged in every way, and in my mind I had passed every test. Many times I had been so close to breaking, but I held on, even if just barely. I had experienced a lifetime of emotions, from exhilaration to despair to intense camaraderie to vicious hatred. When I came home I had no way of working through the confusion. I had no one to talk to who understood. So I just drove the feelings deeper and never talked about them. On my own, I blended back into society and excelled. I graduated from college with a business degree in three years. I worked hard and started my own company, and I have done well. The marines taught me the skills and discipline to achieve a certain amount of success outwardly, but inside I was anything but successful. I grew bitter, resentful, and cynical. The fury of the war lived right below the surface, and at the least provocation the anger came flowing out.

In my most private thoughts, I still fought the war. Any tenderness in my heart had died in Vietnam. I was numb. My feelings died with the marines on the battlefield.

◆   ◆   ◆

Now after many years, I sat in the quietness of my office and was determined to forgive America for not serving me that meal. I reached for the old yellowing airplane ticket lying on my desk and threw it into the trash. I had held on to the anger long enough. Throwing the ticket away was a beginning.

I realized that the war was really over. I'd never be asked to serve my country again, and there was nothing I could do to change anything that I did or that had been done to me. I had to either move on with my life and accept my fate or just become more resentful and bitter. No longer would I treat the ones that I loved most like members of my squad, demanding perfection from them—no excuses, hump your load, get with the program! I was trying to make sure that they would make it, survive the war of life, but I was only driving them farther and farther away. How could they understand what I'd been through? It was impossible for them to know. From now on, I'd smother them with all of the love that I had left to give. No more torment or harsh words and snarls of rage hurled at them in anger. Maybe they would find it in their hearts to forgive me. War had done it to me; it had turned me into the hard and demanding person that I had become. Maybe by letting go of my war I could once again become a facsimile of the loving kid that I once was when I was nineteen, enjoying whatever life threw at me, carefree and accepting. Just maybe I could find some of the precious innocence that was stolen from me when I was given a rifle and told to kill. I prayed that I could.

◆   ◆   ◆

Months went by, and then my son Brian, who was on active duty in the Marine Corps, called and told us that his squad had won the Marine Corps Super Squad Competition and that he would be awarded a medal by the commandant of the Marine Corps at the Marine Corps Barracks located at Eighth and I in Washington, D.C. What a tremendous honor. There was no way I would miss the event.

The commandant's barracks was built around a vast grass parade deck, and in typical Marine Corps fashion, on the night of the event everything was spit-shined and polished. The area was stunning in the golden glow of dusk, the sky awash in pink and gray. A slight summer breeze drifted through the stands. Nettie and I took our seats as the evening darkness began to settle over the crowd.

A spotlight shone on a flagpole atop one of the two-story barracks as two marines slowly moved into position, preparing to raise the flag. The Marine Corps Band, requiring no command to achieve perfect synchronization, marched onto the parade deck. Then, as the American flag was raised slowly and deliberately in the spotlight, strains of the national anthem filled the night air.

I automatically snapped to attention, my heart filled with pride and my eyes filled with tears. I was a marine again!

To my amazement, the Marine of Honor that night was General Chapman, the retired commandant whose name I recited hundreds of times in boot camp while Gunny screamed at us. To my further surprise, one of the other squads being honored that night was from my old unit, Fox 2/5.

My heart filled with a father's pride when my son marched on to that field and the commandant of the Marine Corps pinned his medal over his heart. I realized that my life as a marine had come from feeling abandoned and neglected, confused and bitter, to feeling the satisfaction and pride of being a marine.

As the members of Fox 2/5 marched onto the field to receive their honor, I thought of my buddies who deserved to be honored, and I visualized them on the field, standing tall and having a medal pinned to their chest—Bove, Opossum, Boyd, Donnie, Tennessee, Canada, Anderson, Lee, Starkey, Doc Seely, Koonce, Trenn, Bolby, Lt. Maley, Deane, and all the other marines I served with.

As I watched the ceremony, I realized why I had been so angry and confused for so many years. I listened to the crowd as they clapped and cheered for these marines. Now I understood perfectly. The cruel truth became obvious. America only accepts winners, and in the eyes of America, Vietnam was a loser, and those who fought were losers.

I can never change how America feels about my war and the soldiers who fought it. The soldiers of Vietnam will never be honored. It's too late for that. But I can wash away the bitterness of war that consumed my life.

As a marine in Vietnam, I loved my country and served with honor to the best of my ability, and that would have to be good enough. I did not fail, and I need not feel shame for the failure of others. I asked God to forgive me for the evil things I did in the heat of battle, and I knew that I was forgiven. I need not ask anyone else. I wasn't responsible for Vietnam; America was. I and hundreds of thousands of other soldiers fought the battle for them.

The public watched the war on TV every night, becoming increasingly sick and tired of death and suffering. They tired of hearing the screams and watching the blood flow into the mud, so they turned away. Every time the public looked at us, we reminded them of their failure, and they didn't like what they saw, so the country turned their backs on us.

War is always vicious and merciless and tears at our country's foundation, causing us to question our judgment. In times of war, we look inward, waving Old Glory in the face of our youth to stir the patriotism that we as Americans have tucked tightly in our gut. But, we need a sound reason, more than pride and the desire to dominate other nations, to justify sending our nation's precious soldiers into the abyss of war, forcing them to listen to the loathsome sound of lead smashing into flesh, the haunting, horrible thud of death, and the moans that always follow.

As I watched the ceremony end, tears ran down my face, and I felt that my long war had ended as well. As the lone marine stood on the roof playing "Taps," my wounds were being healed. Without knowing it, the marine was not just closing the ceremony, but he was also saluting my fallen heroes and my memories of war.

◆   ◆   ◆

We didn't get to say good-bye to our fallen friends. They were quickly loaded onto choppers for a race against death. I needed to say good-bye now. I decided to go to the Vietnam Memorial while in Washington.

As I approached the memorial, a warm breeze blew through the trees, and the sun cast the shadows of dancing leaves on the winding path that led to the wall. Like a hushed church congregation, the crowd stood or knelt in reverent silence. I dreaded walking up to the awesome monument, whose dark black sloping wings reminded me of a sinister B-52 bomber.

I felt the deep pain of war once again. War caused the loved ones of these precious soldiers to clutch photos of their fallen sons and daughters, rocking back and forth, crying for their loss wondering, "What if?"

As I stood before the monument, I remembered their faces and I found their names. I slowly reached out and placed my fingers into the engraved stone, then rested my forehead against the cold black marble. I was attending the funeral of my fallen heroes. Silently, I said a prayer for all who fell in war.

When I stood in front of Bove's name, I remembered the pledge I had made so many years before. I knew that I had to visit his mother. I would hold her in my arms and whisper softly to her about what a fine young man her son had been and how much his friendship meant to me during the worst days of my life. He made me laugh when I wanted to cry. He gave me strength when I felt like quitting, and he found hope in the midst of darkness. I could face his mother now without the bitterness and guilt of living while Bove had so tragically died.

As I walked away from the wall, I felt the pain lifting and fading into the past. Now I accepted that I was blessed to be alive. I would honor the dead by appreciating the joys of life.

Also, a strange thing occurred. I thought of the young NVA that I so violently killed. I had let my horrifying, ghastly acts of battle slip into the past, like a nomadic spirit drifting into space, and suddenly I knew that the hideous act that I dreamed about for years was not so painful anymore.

My war in Vietnam was finally over.

Epilogue

I would keep my promise to Bove. When I returned home, it took me a while to find Bove's mother. Her husband had died years earlier, and she had remarried. Thankfully she was still living. I called her. She was delighted to hear from me, since Bove had often written of our friendship, and when I told her of the pledge that Harmon and I had made the night before leaving to go to Vietnam, she insisted that I come to Vermont. I realized that my visit would cause discomfort for both of us and that all the old memories we both had would come flowing from the painful past, but I had to go.

I landed in Boston and rented a car for the drive to Burlington. Nettie came with me. We weaved down the winding roads of Vermont. It was November, and a light snow shower that fell the night before left wispy snow on the ground, and the cold fall wind blew the dusty snow from the tall evergreen trees, swirling it across the road.

The directions were easy and I soon found myself in front of her house. Her son, Perry, lived right next door, and he was the first to greet me. I couldn't believe how much he looked like Harmon. He had the same walk, that same cocky bounce in his step, and I immediately remembered Bove as he turned his back on me in An Hoa to report to his unit and flippantly raised his hand and shot me the bird. I shook Perry's hand and we embraced.

"Dark," Perry said in the same haunting voice that was Harmon's, "Harmon wrote often of you. You were a good friend. Thank you for coming." I was relieved. We instantly bonded. "Mother is next door, and she is waiting for you." He led me to the front door. I had faced all the nightmares of war, looked into death's eyes, but in a way these next few steps would be as tough as anything I ever did in war.

Perry opened the door and there, sitting next to the fire, was Harmon's mother, Irene. She was wrapped in a shawl. She rose from her chair, and we hugged like I had known her all of my life. She sank back into her chair, and I sat on the sofa next to her, and we made meaningless small talk about kids and life in general. We talked about Harmon, and she told me her now infamous stories about him, and I pictured each one in my head as she tossed her head and laughed at herself.

We talked for an hour or so about the war but mostly about the good times spent with Harmon. I hesitated to leave, sensing that I'd never see her again. But it was time to go to the cemetery to visit Harmon's grave.

The biting cold air mixed with falling snow, and the damp dreary clouds formed a misty fog that settled over the town. As I walked to the car, I turned to see Irene standing at the window, meekly waving. I returned the wave and took my last glance at her. How powerful my time with her had been. Bove would have been proud. Then we drove away. It was a Sunday morning, and Burlington was still asleep. The ride was like a funeral procession. The cemetery was next to the baseball field that Harmon played so well on in high school. A monument was raised in his honor to acknowledge his athletic accomplishments, and I realized how much his death had affected the community.

As we drove through the winding streets in the cemetery, large maple trees stood leafless as if guarding the grounds, and I imagined how beautiful and peaceful it must be in the warm days of summer. It was a good place for Harmon to be buried.

I arrived at his grave. The stonemasons in Burlington had made his headstone. It resembled a bench in the dugout, with a baseball and glove etched into the stone, as if Harmon would, from time to time, slip on the glove and walk to the baseball field just down the hill and take his position in the outfield.

For a few seconds I just stood looking at his gravestone, and I realized that there were no guarantees in life. Life never promises that we will die for the right reasons, in the best of circumstances, or at an appropriate time. Now that I was aging, every day getting closer to death, I almost envied Bove in an odd way, because he will always remain that youthful, exuberant young man, frozen in time and etched in everyone's minds that way, a hero forever.

As I stood at his grave I sensed real peace for the first time. In my heart I knew that *no matter what war America sends its soldiers to fight in, and regardless of the reasons they are sent, American soldiers never die in vain.* Every precious son or daughter who has died in battle did so for America, and there is honor in that. America will always be able to find young men and women to fight her battles and die for her glory—she need only ask.

I knelt by his grave. "Harmon, it took me a long time, but I came to visit your family, my friend. I realize now that the time has not been right before now. I was so bitter, Harmon. Losing you and my other marine buddies made me so very hard and resentful. I understand now why you wanted me to come to Burlington. Being with your family has given me such peace, and I think your mother feels the same contentment that I now carry in my heart. Thank you, my friend, for always being there for me. I'll always miss you. I'm going to leave you now and try to lock all the painful memories into the past, where they belong. But I'll never forget you or what you did for America. I'm going to live a good life, Bove. I'll live my life in honor of you."

I stood at attention and gave him a salute. "And God bless America!"

The End

978-0-595-45893-6
0-595-45893-9

Printed in the United States
134827LV00002B/334/A

9 780595 458936